The
Front Yard Forager

The
Front Yard Forager

*Identifying, Collecting,
and Cooking the
30 Most Common
Urban Weeds*

MELANY VORASS HERRERA

SKIPSTONE

DEDICATION

With tremendous affection and gratitude
to my husband, Carlos Herrera,
for his constant love, support, encouragement,
and wise counsel.

Published by Skipstone, an imprint of The Mountaineers Books

Printed in the United States of America
16 15 14 13   5 4 3 2 1
Copy Editor: Kris Fulsaas
Design: Jane Jeszeck, Jigsaw / www.jigsawseattle.com
All photographs by author unless credited otherwise.
Cover photographs: clockwise from top left: *Wild Fennel Cookies; wild carrot flowers; the author foraging in her neighborhood* (Photo by Celia Martí Herrera); *shotweed.*

Library of Congress Cataloging-in-Publication Data
Herrera, Melany Vorass.
The front yard forager : identifying, collecting, and cooking the 30 most common urban weeds
in urban North America / by Melany Vorass Herrera. — 1st ed.
     p. cm.
  Includes bibliographical references and index.
  ISBN 978-1-59485-747-8 (trade paper : alk. paper) — ISBN 978-1-59485-748-5 (ebook)
1. Weeds—United States—Identification. 2. Weeds—North America—Identification. 3. Wild plants, Edible—United States. 4. Wild plants, Edible—North America. 5. Urban plants—United States. 6. Urban plants—North America. 7. Cooking (Wild foods) I. Title.
  SB612.A2V67 2013
  581.6'52—dc23

                  2013005372

ISBN (paperback): 978-1-59485-747-8
ISBN (ebook): 978-1-59485-748-5
Skipstone books may be purchased for corporate, educational, or other promotional sales.
For special discounts and information, contact our Sales Department at 800-553-4453
or mbooks@mountaineersbooks.org.
Skipstone
1001 SW Klickitat Way, Suite 201
Seattle, Washington 98134
206.223.6303
www.skipstonebooks.org
www.mountaineersbooks.org

LIVE LIFE. MAKE RIPPLES.

CONTENTS

INTRODUCTION: A Passion for Weeds

The fields and hills are a table constantly spread.
—Henry David Thoreau

've enjoyed foraging for wild foods as far back as I can remember, and I've long had a fondness for the pleasant countenance of a weed. Though I occasionally found opportunities to combine these interests, I was familiar with only a handful of edible weeds and didn't eat them regularly.

But when Katrina, a category 3 hurricane, hit the Gulf Coast, I read many stories about victims suffering from lack of food, stories often accompanied by photos of people surrounded by edible urban weeds. The stories and photos gave me pause. While I tend not to worry incessantly about natural disasters, I do live in an area prone to major earthquakes, a couple of which I've experienced. Geologists tell us the Pacific Northwest is overdue for a massive quake. What would happen if Seattle were cut off from the rest of the world for a couple of weeks, I wondered. Would I be able to take care of myself and my loved ones? And so began my interest in urban foraging.

The more I learned about these humble gifts from nature, the more my motivation evolved beyond simple survivalism. Today, flavor, nutrition, saving time, and environmental concerns all contribute to my love of weed cuisine.

It seems strange that we don't all have at least a basic understanding about the edible plants around us. My husband and I raise urban dairy goats, and I enjoy watching the does patiently teach their kids what to eat. In fact, many mammals teach their young what they can eat from nature. We seem to be the only species that has forgotten how essential it is for our children to learn how to feed themselves.

But parents can't teach what they don't know, so we need to refresh our collective memories by refamiliarizing ourselves with some of these vital plants—by reading books like this one, by taking workshops, and by teaching one another.

With this book, I want readers to:

- Know how simple, fun, and satisfying it is to identify and cook with the edible weeds most common to our urban areas.
- Reconsider the notion that all weeds are bad and should be eliminated.
- Reflect on the implications of a species that has forgotten how to feed itself from nature.
- Personally enjoy the benefits of the ultimate locavore experience—eating the weeds in your own yard and neighborhood.

Acknowledgments

With gratitude to my mother and grandmothers who, with their strong-willed, resourceful, and self-sufficient natures, were all impressive examples of female strength. I am also deeply thankful to my father for his unconditional love and steady support of everything I do, and for humoring me by eating and apparently enjoying the yucca blossom I offered him last summer.

Grateful recognition and a few apologies go to my immediate and extended families for willingly(?) playing guinea pig to my cooking experiments. Special thanks to my stepson, Noah, for taking care of logistics on many a foraging excursion, as well as for keeping a smile on my face nearly all of the time with his loving presence. Also, a hardy note of appreciation to my awesome sibs Margot Vorass, Mark Vorass, Jim Vorass, and Gail Robert, and my cousin Steve Vorass who, for more than twenty years, have enthusiastically told me, "You really should write," as well as for their (mostly) tasteful humor and teasing.

For their steady encouragement and support, I greatly appreciate the strong and capable women in my life: Rachel Baker, Bev Cousineau, Michelle Cramer, Rebecca Dare, Melleoux d'Estres, Kris Geringer, Gaye Grindrod, Georgia Hancock, Heather Graham, Suzanne Mackey, Sarah Moore, Lynn Mueller, Sr. Mary Ann O'Mara, Kathy Morris, Sue Patnude, Lisa Prigmore, Diane Robertson, Sally-Anne Sadler, Laura St. Clair Klein, Theresa Wood, and Myra Gallier Zocher.

Many thanks to Carey Thornton for scheduling my first formal urban foraging classes, to Seattle Tilth for allowing me to continue them, and to the many other organizations that have hosted my classes. I'm also grateful for all the encouragement and support I received from my fellow author friends, Anne Biklé, John Gastil, Jennie Palches Grant, Annette Cottrell, Josh McNichols, Jennifer Katzinger, David Montgomery, and Cindy Simmons.

I wish to express my gratitude to the writers who helped deepen my awareness of the sacred relationship we enjoy with the food we eat, including Wendell Berry, Sepp Holzer, Bill Mollison, Gary Nabhan, Michael Pollan, Eric Schlosser, Timothy Lee Scott, and Vandana Shiva.

I am also most grateful to the many foraging experts whose writings and videos helped inform this book, including Steve Brill, Francois Couplan, Green Dean, James Duke, Peter Dykeman, Thomas Elias, Euell Gibbons, John Kallas, Linda Runyon, and Samuel Thayer.

I owe a debt of gratitude to the many mentors and professionals who helped shape this project, among them, Skipstone's editor in chief, Kate Rogers, for recognizing the uniqueness of this book's subject and for candidly sharing her wisdom throughout the writing process, as well as senior editor Mary Metz and copy editor Kris Fulsaas, for magically transforming my draft into a coherent, cogent piece of writing.

Finally, deep gratitude to the fine teachers who so generously fed my love of reading, writing, biology, ethnobotany, and public policy: Francis Woski, Kate Crow, Jack Kriegl, Marja Eloheimo, and Linda Moon-Stumpf, respectively.

Recipes for the Front Yard Forager

1 | GETTING STARTED WITH FRONT YARD FORAGING

for·age [Middle English, from Old French *fourrage,* from *forrer,* "to forage," from *feurre,* "fodder," of Germanic origin] *n.* 1. Food for domestic animals; fodder. 2. The act of looking or searching for food or provisions. *v. intr.* 1. To wander in search of food or provisions. 2. To make a raid, as for food: *soldiers foraging near an abandoned farm.* 3. To conduct a search; rummage. *v. tr.* 1. To collect forage from; strip of food or supplies: *troops who were foraging the countryside.* 2. *Informal:* To obtain by foraging: *foraged a snack from the refrigerator.*

—*The American Heritage Dictionary of the English Language,* fourth edition

Oh, humble weed
How do I love thee?
Let me count the ways…

– with apologies to Elizabeth Barrett Browning

Urban foraging is a fun and satisfying challenge. Learning the names and uses of new plants is enriching and rewarding. It's a great way to transform an urban sidewalk stroll into a refreshing nature hike.

REASONS TO FORAGE FOR WEEDS

Why do I have such an affection for weeds? There are *so* many reasons! Here are a few reasons why you should give them a try too.

Enjoy a New Activity

Experience nature. Harvesting urban weeds helps us develop a closer relationship with the environment we live, work, and play in. Once you learn how to identify a particular plant, you begin to see it everywhere. Knowing these edibles helps you to realize how amazingly abundant our planet is.

Find personal satisfaction. Harvesting weeds gives you a deep sense of satisfaction you don't get when you shop at the grocery store.

Get fresh air and exercise. Foraging for urban weeds allows you to get some moderate outdoor exercise. Your body feels much better when you take a short walk outdoors each day.

Eat Healthily

Weeds are free! Even if your diet is nearly all organic, the grocery store cost sometimes is at odds with frugality. When you carefully select foraging areas, you know you're getting high-quality organic food for significantly less cost in time *and* money than it takes to drive to the store, walk the aisles in search of decent food, stand in line, return home, and unpack groceries.

Weeds let you eat locally. It doesn't get any more local than your front yard. Unlike the foods in our grocery stores or even at the local farmers market, weeds do not have to be transported in your vehicle. Their carbon footprint registers as zero!

Weeds are fresh food. Foraged food is freshly picked. A number of studies conclude nutritional value is greatly diminished after harvest. A study by the Institute for Food Research demonstrates that, on average, vegetables lose 45% of their nutritional value between harvest time and consumption. For example, spinach stored at room temperature loses up to 90% of its vitamin C within 24 hours of being picked; when refrigerated, it loses 75% of its vitamin C within seven days of harvest. A "yard to mouth" diet gives optimum nutrition.

You will never catch me with a sign like this in my yard. Weeds have too many great uses for me to simply give them away!

Weeds are beyond nutritious. Most weeds pack a *much* more powerful punch than our store-bought vegetables do. Eating a wild green salad gives you a pick-me-up much like a cup of coffee does.

Weeds are preventive medicine. Most of the weeds in this book are credited with some medicinal value. When you consume these foraged foods as a regular part of your diet, you're consuming high quantities of preventive medicine.

Grow Your Own

Build up the soil. Weeds add organic matter through living mulches. They are pioneers of disturbed earth that repair degraded land, prevent erosion, reduce soil salinity, and create shade for the next stage of forest growth. Taprooted weeds benefit shallower-rooted plants (like garden lettuce) by bringing nutrients up from deeper soils.

This plant, known as honesty or money plant, is a close relative to broccoli. Like broccoli, it's packed with healthy antioxidants and contains nutrients that help prevent cancer. Unlike broccoli, it doesn't require assistance and comes free of charge.

Use weeds as garden pest traps. Some weeds attract predator insects, so you can use the weeds as pest control in your conventional vegetable garden. Today, I allow weeds to thrive near my yard and garden. I've even started a vegetable bed dedicated to my weedy friends.

Weeds are anything but labor intensive. Weeds are the lazy gardener's dream come true! You don't have to till soil, provide irrigation, add soil amendments, or do any weeding. Weeds stand up to the most brutal punishment and, in fact, seem to enjoy being regularly trampled.

Grow a healthy lawn and habitat. Weeds make lawns more diverse and healthy. Clover is an excellent nitrogen fixer, and taproots bring nutrients up to boost the health of shallower soils. A wild lawn attracts a greater variety of butterflies and birds than a manicured lawn will.

Weedy lawns are good for bare feet. You will love walking barefoot on your taller, weed-friendly lawn because it's much softer than short-mown grass.

Have time for other fun stuff. If you let your lawn grow long to accommodate better weed growth, you can do other fun things instead of spending hours behind a mower.

A BRIEF HISTORY OF WEEDS

> *And what is a weed?*
> *A plant whose virtues have not yet*
> *been discovered.*

—Ralph Waldo Emerson, *Fortune of the Republic*

With all of their benefits, how did weeds fall from favor? Most plants we call weeds today were at one time considered beneficial plants. In fact, many were intentionally brought by immigrants to North America as food and medicine.

One hundred fifty years ago, the United States was mainly a rural society. Most adults knew the names and uses of a number of common roadside weeds. During the industrial revolution, however, a large percentage of the population moved to the cities. Many people were physically removed from the plants they once knew and used. Over time, these life-sustaining plants were gradually left behind in favor of newer hybrids transported from farm to

My neighbor has the right idea with this sign: We should all be this proud of our weeds!

city markets. These plants were often larger and more colorful than anything in the wild.

However, people unable to afford store-bought vegetables or who lived too far away from stores to purchase their groceries continued to eat wild plants. Sadly, because wild plants were generally eaten by the less wealthy, foraged foods came to be considered inferior, certainly unworthy of the middle-class dining-room table. Today plants that our great-grandparents and their ancestors actively cultivated or sought for food and medicine are the very "weeds" we now spend billions trying to eradicate.

It is very human to wish to control nature. It's practically what defines our species. But we've become downright neurotic in our insistence on controlling weeds. We go to extraordinary lengths to dominate plants we've decided don't belong. Yet, with all the blood, sweat, and tears we've poured into the task, we've made very little headway.

We are in classic denial about the fact that we're losing our war on weeds. We have this illusory feeling of being able to control them, but it is becoming more and more evident that we have only a fleeting influence.

For example, most of us feel that we must keep our front lawns green, mown short, and weed free. We've become so accustomed to the expectation of a tidy front yard that to question or depart from that behavior feels completely foreign to us.

Why do we want this hypercontrol? Why are weeds such an issue with us? I think our war on weeds boils down to three areas we wish to defend and protect:

- the American lawn
- industrial agriculture
- native species

Sometimes our efforts can be considered valiant. But for the most part, the punishment we exact on weeds does not fit the crime, especially given all they have to offer us.

Weed War I: Protecting the All-American Lawn

Most of our homes feature a front yard comprised almost entirely of grass, yet people seldom sit on, play in, or enjoy their front lawns. Yes, most building codes require a setback from the road or street, and yes, lawn is considered the easiest way to fill that space. But why do we insist on our manicured, weed-free lawns?

A LABOR-INTENSIVE NEW GARDENING STYLE

In *The Lawn: A History of an American Obsession*, Virginia Scott Jenkins tells us that lawns started appearing in France in the 1700s, initially as part of a formal French gardening style created and popularized by landscape architect André Le Nôtre at the Palace of Versailles. As England adopted the French style, an English "lawn" came to mean a portion of garden or playground covered with manicured grass.

The word lawn didn't enter the American lexicon until the late 18th century and likely did not become an everyday word until well after the Civil War, when suburbanization became a trend. Before that time, yards were usually small gardens surrounded by uncultivated native grasses. In the South where lawn grasses were especially difficult to grow, front yards were usually swept, packed dirt.

But by the late 18th century, the European landscaping trend caught on in America, and wealthy landowners with plenty of hired help began keeping lawns. Doing his best to imitate the newer English gardens, for instance, George Washington hired English gardeners at Mount Vernon. According to Jenkins, when Washington died, reproductions of his Mount Vernon tomb were distributed throughout the United States, introducing the masses to the concept of a grass lawn.

Still, ordinary Americans had no interest in keeping a lawn because it was expensive and labor intensive. Nonetheless, by the early 1900s, architectural design books began showing homes surrounded by lawn instead of gardens perhaps because it distracted less from the home. Jenkins suggests the lawn may have become established with the middle class as a result of these books. New landscaping styles in public parks as well as golf's increasing popularity also contributed to more lawns.

Once push lawnmowers appeared in the late 1800s, the grassy lawn became much more accessible to the middle class. Eventually, lawnmowers were quite affordable, and middle-class Americans were able to imitate gardens they'd seen in books and postcards. Lawns became a symbol of wealth.

CHEMICAL WARFARE

After the Second World War, there was great commercial interest in converting weapons of chemical warfare into fertilizers and pesticides. Dow, Dupont, Monsanto, and other chemical companies that had recently stockpiled chemical arsenals now diligently promoted the weed-free lawn through the application of such chemicals as phenyl mercury acetate, potassium cyanate, arsenicals, 2,4-D (Agent Orange), DDT, dieldrin, chloropicrin (tear gas), chlordane, and ammonium sulfate.

By the 1950s, the new chemical fertilizers and pesticides—as well as imported grasses, improved lawnmowers, and irrigation—made it possible for most people to grow lawns in most parts of the United States. Front lawns became a standard feature of the middle-class home.

As Jenkins points out, today our lawn habit supports a multibillion-dollar lawn-care industry. Front lawn standards were established for suitable types of grass, color, and upkeep. In 1962 Rachel Carson's *Silent Spring* noted that "every hardware store, garden-supply shop, and supermarket has rows of insecticides for every conceivable horticultural situation." In spite of Carson's warnings, by the 1980s, Americans largely accepted the grass lawn's

dependence on chemicals. It became common to see "herbicide" signs placed in lawns by companies such as Chemlawn, the Lawn Doctor, and TruGreen.

In 1986 the National Cancer Institute issued a study that linked several lawn chemicals to health problems including cancer, birth defects, miscarriages, male infertility, liver failure, kidney dysfunction, and fetal death, as well as extreme toxicity to fish and other aquatic life. In 1989 the National Academy of Sciences stated that homeowners tend to use up to 10 times more chemicals per acre on their lawns than farmers use on agricultural land.

Since the 1986 study, the use of lawn care pesticides has decreased to some degree. But we still have very high expectations of our green carpets. Most cities have grass height restrictions and prohibitions on noxious weeds.

By the 1990s, landscaping magazines suggested it might be acceptable to have a few weeds in the lawn. Now a growing number of people say no to pesticide use on their

Wild carrot (or Queen Anne's lace) is considered an agricultural pest in many states; overuse of chemical controls has made it resistant to many herbicides.

Once a lawn is allowed to grow 6 to 8 inches, all kinds of tasty food plants suddenly appear.

with green spray paint. During prolonged droughts, some companies even perform such a service.

Artificial turf is another solution for a maintenance- and irrigation-free lawn. One of my neighbors recently converted her parking strip from vegetable garden to artificial turf.

Some folks who don't like using industrial chemicals spend much time and effort ridding their yard of weeds by using a gas torch or applying vinegar.

Our love affair with the weed-free green lawn is a habit, just one of those neurotic remnants from the past that makes very little sense for today.

Weed War II: Protecting Industrial Agriculture

Weed: any plant that poses a major threat to agriculture and/or natural ecosystems within the United States.

—US Department of Agriculture

lawns, and natural lawns and backyard wilderness sanctuaries have become popular.

Nevertheless, some sources suggest that even today Americans are spending about $40 billion a year on lawn maintenance, much of it for weed control chemicals.

OTHER IMPACTS

Another problem related to maintaining grass lawns is disposal of grass clippings. Many municipalities call for bagging and disposing of those clippings, which comprise up to 50 percent of the nation's quickly disappearing landfill capacity.

We also use enormous quantities of water to keep our grass lawns green. The federal Environmental Protection Agency estimates nearly a third of all residential water use in the country goes toward lawn upkeep. Lawn grass requires an inch of water per week, meaning that a 25-by-40-foot lawn needs about 10,000 gallons of water per summer.

Even those who don't use chemicals or exorbitant amounts of water find ways to achieve the formal green lawn. Here in Seattle, when drought conditions result in water restrictions, some folks paint their dry, yellow grass

According to a 1999 Cornell University study, the United States spends about $10 billion per year pouring 1.1 billion pounds of more than 600 different pesticides onto our food crops for agricultural weed control. Indirect costs (for example, public health impacts, pesticide-resistant weeds, crop loss, and impacts on birds, fish, honeybees, and groundwater) add an estimated $12 billion per year.

HERBICIDE-RESISTANT WEEDS

Yet herbicide-resistant weeds are a growing concern; we can no longer eradicate these plants with chemical herbicides.

Several crops, including corn, soybeans, and beets, have been genetically modified to withstand heavy applications of the herbicide glyphosate (Roundup), the use of which theoretically allows farmers to eradicate weeds while leaving crop plants unharmed. However, according to a 2008 study by Baden Aniline and Soda Factory, Bayer, Dow, Dupont, Monsanto, Syngenta, the US Department of Agriculture (USDA), and various agricultural associations, many weeds are or are becoming resistant to glyphosate.

Interestingly, of the six weeds the report lists as glyphosate resistant, all of them are edible, some having been used as crop plants in our past and some still being used as crop plants in other countries. A report in 2006 by Hugh J. Beckie lists 11 plants as the most common genera of weeds developing herbicide resistance. Except for two plants on this list, all are edible and many, such as amaranth and lamb's-quarter, are more nutritious than some of the crops they're removed from.

Because herbicide manufacturers' plans for "Roundup ready" crops have begun to fail, in 2012 they requested USDA's fast-track approval for additional genetically modified organisms (GMOs) to keep agricultural crops growing in the face of 2,4-D (Agent Orange) and dicamba applications. The success of such an approach is highly dubious: 2,4-D- and dicamba-resistant weeds were reported as early as 1945.

As additional GMOs are approved, millions more pounds of toxic herbicides will be sprayed, polluting our food, groundwater, surface water, soil, and air and causing untold harm to farmworkers. However, weed scientists continue to operate as though herbicide resistance is a problem that can easily be overcome by applying ever newer and more toxic herbicides.

Weed resistance is such a concern that we now employ whole armies of degreed weed scientists. Some of them sit on a national Weed Taskforce; others staff National Weed Summits. We have an Herbicide Resistance Action Committee, a Weed Science Society of America, and a North American Herbicide Resistance Action Committee. All these organizations exist to successfully exact genocide on a few unwanted plants; most seem to be in the business of promoting chemical herbicide application. And to what end?

LESS-NUTRITIOUS FOOD CROPS

The small number of fruits and vegetables we've deemed acceptable grocery store products are less nutritious now than ever. Industrial food crops, whether hybrids or genetically modified, are produced for color, size, and shelf life rather than nutritional value.

A 2005 study by Donald Davis, Melvin Epp, and Hugh Riordan of 50 years of USDA food analysis data found declines in six key nutrients: 9 percent less iron, 6 percent less protein, 16 percent less calcium, 9 percent less phosphorus, 15 percent less iron, 38 percent less vitamin B2, and 20 percent less vitamin C. The study also showed reductions in magnesium, zinc, copper, and selenium. These genetic tradeoffs, called *dilution effects,* are further compounded by increasing the size and rates of yield through fertilization and irrigation, according to Nyle Brady's 1981 *Advances in Agronomy.*

We are now eating fruits and vegetables that offer more pesticide residues and less flavor than anything we've consumed in our entire history. Numerous studies link pesticides with cancer, birth defects, and organ failure.

LOST TOPSOIL

Our careless agricultural practices are also resulting in an ever-accelerating rate of topsoil loss. Two hundred years ago, agricultural land in most of the United States was overlain with about 21 inches of topsoil. That number today is just over a few inches. Some estimate that the United States has already lost more than 70 percent of one of its most precious natural resources.

Currently, the United States loses another inch of topsoil about every 16 years, according to John Robbins in *Healthy at 100: The Scientifically Proven Secrets of the World's Healthiest and Longest Lived People.* At that rate, we will have completely depleted our topsoil reserves within another hundred years—and it takes about 500 years for an inch of topsoil to accumulate. As David R. Montgomery points out in *Dirt: The Erosion of Civilizations,* in human history wherever agricultural practices resulted in continued soil erosion, civilizations have gone extinct.

Sadly, what topsoil does remain is virtually dead as a result of years of pesticide and chemical fertilizer application—that is, it lacks the microbes that plants rely on to effectively absorb nutrients from the soil.

All these problems mean we need to find better ways to grow our food. A growing number of respected scientists acknowledge that our experiment with modern agriculture is failing us.

Weed War III: Protecting Native Species

Calling a plant invasive allows us to blame it for ruining the environment when really . . . weeds are the symptoms of environmental degradation, not the cause. Casting such plants in the role of thugs makes it virtually impossible to recognize the positive contributions they are making to the ecology of cities.

—Peter Del Tredici,
Wild Urban Plants of the Northeast

The USDA defines a native species as a plant that is "a part of the balance of nature that has developed over hundreds or thousands of years in a particular region or ecosystem." According to the USDA, only plants that were found in this country before European settlement (1492) are considered native to the United States. Invasive species are defined by the USDA as nonnative (or alien) to the ecosystem and causing or likely to cause economic or environmental harm or harm to human health.

Thus, invasive species are considered one of the largest threats to our endangered natives. While this may be true, isn't that the way it's supposed to work? Isn't evolution

When Seattle's rain dries up for the summer, so do people's grass lawns. But drought tolerant weeds continue to thrive. This patch of clover looks like a lush oasis in the middle of a desert of parched lawn.

about survival of the fittest? Or should Earth be as static as we can make it? I can almost hear environmentalists crying "Heresy!" with arguments like "Yes, but this rapid migration wasn't what the universe intended, and it's only because we humans have interrupted nature."

Apparently, we know more about the intentions of the universe than the universe does, and we've decided that humans and their activities are not part of nature. This line of thinking contributes to the delusion that we're able to bring everything back into check by applying external controls, like toxic chemical applications, to fix everything.

A STATIC OR DYNAMIC UNIVERSE?

According to Nina-Marie Lister, in a 2012 online interview about the book *Ecological Urbanism*, as experts research whole ecosystems, the biological sciences are moving toward a model that is more open-ended, flexible, and resilient than our historical approach of stability and control. Lister and others now suggest that ecosystems are self-organizing and unpredictable and that dynamic change is built into any system that is truly alive.

Old-school biology and ecology taught us that ecosystems gradually reach climax states from which they don't move unless disturbed by some external force. But Lister points out that ecosystems are constantly evolving, sometimes unevenly.

It's true that we impact the ecosystems in which we live, sometimes permanently. But managing for environmental stasis is not only unrealistic but most unnatural. We would do much better to manage our own behaviors rather than trying to control the rate at which ecosystems change.

BENEFITS OF WILD URBAN PLANTS

Even though, by definition, not all nonnative plants are invasive, the general public now tends to assume that all alien plants are a threat to the environment. As Harvard ecologist Peter Del Tredici points out in *Wild Urban Plants of the Northeast*, our goal of eradicating all nonnative plants in favor of native plants has resulted in completely forgetting the benefits of allowing nonnatives to grow. Del Tredici calls weeds "wild urban plants" and stresses their value in urban settings because they:

- sequester carbon
- break up hardpan soils
- are the first soil colonizers
- reduce topsoil erosion
- fix nitrogen
- filter stormwater
- remediate contamination

Because weeds are opportunists and grow where other plants will not, we assume they are outcompeting and displacing native vegetation. While this may be true of some weeds in some circumstances, in urban environments the damage has already been very well achieved by human activity. We've removed the native vegetation and the native topsoil, raised the urban temperature, and altered the ecosystems of native plants.

While many efforts to reestablish native plants in urban settings are well intended, in such conditions natives are unlikely to survive without constant maintenance. And efforts often run contrary to their aims. Many biologists even use herbicides and import alien species to combat invasive species.

Nitrates, nitrites, and nitrosamines

Most of us associate nitrates and nitrites with elevated levels of cancer risk, even though the 1970s study supporting that concern was later discredited. However, before the study was thrown out, the USDA and FDA restricted the use of nitrates and nitrites in cured meats.

The fact is, you probably ingest far more nitrates from fruits and vegetables than you get from cured meats. This is especially true of leafy greens: many of them greatly exceed the maximum amount allowed in hot dogs and other cured meats. For example, on average butterhead lettuce comes in at 2036 parts per million, beets at 1279 ppm, celery at 1103 ppm, spinach at 1066 ppm, and pumpkin at 874 ppm. The average hot dog contains about 10 ppm. Some experts say that 70 to 95 percent of our nitrate intake is from plants.

In some ways, nitrates are even good for you. Nitrates are absorbed from the gut into the bloodstream, then deposited to the salivary glands. From here, nitrate is secreted into saliva where oral bacteria use it as an energy source, converting it to nitrite. Once ingested, the saliva's nitrite is reabsorbed into the bloodstream where it acts as a vasodilator and reduces blood pressure.

Nitrite is a precursor for nitric oxide, one of the most potent anti-inflammatory and blood vessel-dilating compounds in the body. Scientists now think that a decrease in blood vessel nitric oxide is probably an early consequence of eating a poor diet, perhaps one low in leafy greens.

Nitrosamines, on the other hand, are proven carcinogens. They are formed when nitrates or nitrites form with certain protein amines. However, ascorbic acid (vitamin C) prevents this from happening, and our wonderfully evolved stomachs have plenty of it on hand. People whose stomachs suffer from low acid (hypochloridia) can take supplements to prevent formation of nitrosamine (and other problems associated with low stomach acid).

Throughout the plant descriptions in this book, under the heading Who Should Avoid It, you'll see information on plants that can absorb high levels of nitrate.

Many nonnative weeds, on the other hand, requiring no help whatsoever will:

- combat global warming
- produce oxygen
- provide wildlife habitat
- reclaim abandoned pervious surfaces like paved parking lots

Rather than automatically categorizing these plants as bad, we should recognize and appreciate their potential contribution to the quality of urban life.

A Changing Ecology

According to Mark A. Davis, a plant ecologist who, in a *Scientific American* article by Brendan Borrell, decried potential threats from invasive species, the migration of plants, animals, and other species as a potential that is overhyped by some ecologists. For example, Davis says, buckthorn, garlic mustard, and many other invasive species don't pose nearly as great a threat as many ecologists believe, and we should take measures against invasives only when native plants are directly threatened, noting that nonnative species don't usually drive out native plants. He says that islands and other isolated places are probably the only setting in which invasives can actually cause extinctions.

Both Lister and Davis suggest that we accept that species do not stay put. Michael Pollan put it quite bluntly in a 1994 *New York Times Magazine* essay when he said that turning the ecological clock back to 1492 is futile and pointless. It's important to remember that evolution is a constant, on-going process, not something that only happened "back then" and will happen "in the future."

Is our desire to control weeds worth the time, money, and environmental damage? As the climate continues to warm, we may find ourselves relying on alien species—weeds—to fill vacated niches in our changing ecology. Through our interaction with weeds at the dinner table, we insinuate ourselves into the role of herbivore, creating a very natural, sane means of improving the overall balance of our ever-changing ecosystem. For the sake of the planet and future generations, can we learn to eat, possibly even cultivate, plants that we now call weeds?

THE URBAN FORAGER

This book shows you how simple it is to forage for food in urban environments. But before you race out and gather armloads of weeds, here are a few precautions that urban foragers need to keep in mind.

Safe Foraging

Since the urban forager is providing food from unconventional sources, safety precautions are important.

KNOW THE RISKS OF PLANT POISONING:
POSITIVELY IDENTIFY THE PLANT

Never try to guess at a plant's edibility. Many of us were erroneously told in outdoor programs that if we saw birds eating a plant, we could consider it a safe food. Some of us also remember false aphorisms like "the blacker the berry, the sweeter the juice." Flavor is not a good indicator of plant safety, either; yew berries, also known as death berries, are sweet and juicy, but swallowing the seeds can be fatal.

Just because a berry looks delicious, or you see other animals eating it, doesn't mean it's safe for human consumption. Though bittersweet berries (a.k.a. deadly nightshade) are a shiny, vibrant red, they are toxic to humans.

Poisonous scarlet pimpernel foliage looks similar to that of edible chickweed, but it's easy to tell the difference once you know scarlet pimpernel's blooms are orange while chickweed's are white. *(Photo by Jerry Kirkhart)*

Tasting a plant to determine its edibility, even if you plan to spit it out, is not a good idea either. I didn't know what petty spurge (annual euphorbia) was until I touched a stem to my tongue. It was bitter, so I didn't continue my experiment. About an hour later, the inside of my mouth felt like I'd eaten a bunch of habañero peppers. Petty spurge, it turns out, has such irritating sap that it has been used as a wart remover.

Before gathering a wild plant for the first time, check several foraging books and other published materials. Sometimes reference books and internet sites are incomplete, inaccurate, or contradictory. The Recommended Resources at the end of this book provide some good

Some plants commonly called 'morning glory' are edible while others are not. Learning botanical names reduces the risk of eating something toxic.

Sometimes individuals have sensitivities to plants. Most people are perfectly fine with daylilies, a common food in Japan, while a few people suffer intestinal distress after consuming them. To test, eat only a small portion the first time.

starting points. You can further increase your chances of successfully identifying a plant by taking a class or consulting with an experienced forager.

These are some good rules of thumb for foragers:

- Save several whole specimens: keep two or three whole plants for at least 24 hours after you've eaten your foraged plant, so if you have an adverse reaction you can provide a specimen for positive identification.
- Try only one new plant at a time: don't mix several new species into a recipe, so if you have an adverse reaction you'll know what caused it.
- Try only a small portion at first: if you do have an adverse reaction, it will be less severe if you eat only a tablespoon or two of a new plant on your first try.

My husband and I once learned the hard way. We had been noshing on our parking-strip daylily tubers for several years when one day, after we'd eaten a couple of large helpings, we became violently ill. We weren't certain daylilies were the cause, so a week later we tried them once more, but in a smaller quantity. Sure enough, we were once again ill, only the attack wasn't as fierce as the first one due to the smaller portions.

How could a plant we'd been successfully harvesting for years suddenly make us sick? I pulled out all my books and scoured the internet for an answer, but I wasn't able to find any mention of an experience like ours.

Needless to say, we stopped eating our daylily tubers for a time. Then one day I came across a collection of newsletters written by John Kallas. I learned that Kallas once had an experience identical to ours, though he didn't have a definitive answer as to why this sometimes occurs. Had I done just a little more research on daylilies, I might have read this warning and opted to first test a small amount at the beginning of each season.

As with conventional foods, some individuals have or can develop allergies or sensitivities to a wild food. This also happened to us (it seems we learn all of our lessons the hard way). We'd been enjoying shaggy lepiota mushrooms for several years when we both came down with cases of heartburn that lingered for weeks. It took us awhile to identify the cause, but we finally realized the culprit was the shaggy lepiota. Later, we read that developing a sensitivity or allergy to shaggy lepiota mushrooms is not uncommon.

Also recognize that many plant identification sources erroneously list edible plants as poisonous. I'm glad these sources err on the conservative side, but in many instances these warnings are simply inaccurate. Unfortunately, in the world of foraging, misinformation is often repeated from source to source without much fact-checking. I often see incorrect references to toxicity to humans based on a plant's effect on livestock.

The bottom line? A good forager needs to be willing to spend a little time digging for accurate information.

Parking strips can be great locations for foraging. But it's good to remember that they are also popular locations for 'pottying' pets.

KNOW WHAT TO CALL IT

Ever wonder why scientists use complicated, hard-to-pro-nounce names for familiar plants? Common names such as dandelion and cat's ear convey an immediate idea of what a particular plant looks like, but scientists avoid using them because they are seldom used for a specific species. In North America alone there are at least 16 species of dandelion. To make matters more complicated, individual species often share common names or are given several common names.

To avoid ambiguity and confusion, botanists use binomial nomenclature to identify species. Binomial nomenclature is usually in Latin, with the first name referring to the genus and the second name referring to the species. For example, the scientific name for dandelion is *Taraxacum officinale.*

Although unique, scientific names sometimes change. As improved methods of research provide scientists with more information on a species' evolutionary relationships, its scientific name is sometimes changed to reflect this better understanding. In this book, I list primary common names as well as multiple scientific names when this occurs; my primary source for plant names is the USDA website.

AVOID ENVIRONMENTAL POLLUTION

"You eat weeds that are growing in cities? What about environmental contamination?" While urban contaminants are a reality, in this day and age, environmental contaminants are everywhere. Consider, for example, that polychlorinated biphenyls (PCBs) are found in seals hunted by the Inuit people in the Arctic. However, here are some measures you can take to limit your exposure to urban pollutants.

Be very selective about where you gather wild foods. Do not gather along railroad tracks or next to high-traffic roadsides, places regularly exposed to toxic pesticides, herbicides, heavy metals, and animal waste.

If you collect from areas of standing water, be sure you know where that water traveled from. For instance, I would never collect cattail tubers from a stormwater retention pond. Some plants, such as many in the brassica family, are hyperaccumulators of heavy metals capable of taking up relatively high concentrations of dissolved metals from sources like highway runoff or other stormwater runoff.

But you don't need to be overly cautious. Most plants growing from well-draining soils adjacent to highways do not take up metals. Instead, metals and other particulate matter adhere to the outside of the plant and can be washed off.

Pet waste is not a huge concern either. While it's true that you can't visibly discern whether the plant in question has been urinated upon, urine is typically sterile and is highly unlikely to make you ill. If your plant is growing out of a pile of dog excrement, it's probably best to find another plant because it will be difficult to get that visual out of your mind when you sit down to dinner. However, fecal coliforms are not taken up by plants and can generally be rinsed off and most certainly cooked away.

Don't collect from commercial landscapes; they are nearly always drenched in herbicides. The same can be true for many public parks. Before you harvest, confirm

Know your parking strip. Some people park on them while washing their cars, allowing contaminants to build up on the vegetation. Others apply herbicides.

that your site hasn't been subjected to chemical herbicide applications.

Always thoroughly wash food gathered from urban environments. Even in relatively pristine locations, atmospheric contaminants are deposited area-wide. Soak your harvest in cold water for at least ten minutes, swish it around a couple times, then give it a final rinse in a colander.

BE AWARE OF PERSONAL SAFETY

Pay attention to your surroundings. Stinging insects, hypodermic needles, broken glass, and vehicular traffic are all very real concerns in urban environments.

Also, those wonderfully untended vacant lots filled with edible weeds are often frequented by vagrants. While I'm convinced that most homeless people are just like you and me, some suffer from mental illness and drug addiction, which can lead to violent behavior. Thus it is wise to take appropriate precautions, such as bringing a buddy along.

But there is no need to be overly cautious. I was once asked very threateningly by a homeless man why I was taking his plants. At first I was shaken because I was alone. However, once I told him what I was doing, his face brightened, and he was very eager to learn more.

Responsible Foraging

Just as wild-crafting or -harvesting involves respectful use of natural resources, so does urban foraging, albeit with slightly different concerns.

ASK PERMISSION

Be sure that you have permission from the property owner. Foraging without permission can be considered trespassing and theft, and nobody wants to be arrested for picking a dandelion. Ask the *adjacent* property owner before you pick from a parking strip, since in some jurisdictions, even though these spaces are publicly owned, the adjacent property owner is responsible for them.

I have some personal experience with not asking. One afternoon I decided to make a large dandelion green salad for a dinner gathering that evening. A few blocks from my home, I'd spotted an unmown parking strip in front of what appeared to be a dilapidated old rental building. I thought

Are you quite sure you have permission?

it highly unlikely that anyone would mind me weeding the parking strip, so I did just that. As I gathered up my two- to three-pound harvest I heard a voice behind me say, "Do you think you have enough there?"

At first I thought he was just a passerby teasing me about picking dandelions. But it turned out he owned the adjacent home and for the past ten years had painstakingly dug up dandelions from all over the neighborhood to replant in his own personal dandelion salad garden. I don't blush easily, but I'm sure my face was as deep a red as it gets. I apologized profusely and offered my lootings back to him, but he insisted I take them with me. Lesson learned! I now always, *always* ask.

BE AWARE OF LOCAL REGULATIONS

Legalities related to foraging are not always clear. Many cities have ordinances forbidding the removal of plant material from parks. Don't assume that officials will turn a blind eye to the criminal act of picking a dandelion. A famous (or infamous) forager, Steve Brill, munched down a few dandelions in Central Park in 1986, and two undercover park rangers arrested him on a charge of criminal mischief. He was taken to the station house, fingerprinted, fined, and, after several hours, finally released. (It all ended happily for Brill: Charges were dropped and, in fact, the Parks Department later paid him to lead foraging tours. You may not be so fortunate, however.)

Storing urban weeds

After you've pulled your own greens from your lawn or garden, you can make them last just as long as the store-bought kind with these few tips.

Some greens do well in a cup of water on the counter. Others enjoy an airtight container. Still others do well in an open container in the refrigerator's crisper. However, the method I describe below can be used almost universally with success:

1. Soak the greens in cold water for 10–30 minutes to ensure that they are fully hydrated.
2. Thoroughly rinse and drain greens.
3. Use a salad spinner to remove as much of the surface water as possible.
4. Place the greens on a cutting board and chop them to salad-size pieces.
5. Spread the greens out on clean towels to air dry for one to three hours.
6. Roll the towels up with the greens inside.
7. Secure the rolls with rubber bands.
8. Store in the crisper or bottom shelf of your refrigerator.

When you have a hankering for a salad, unroll just enough greens for your meal, then reroll the towel and secure it once again.

Don't have a salad spinner or one large enough to accommodate your harvest? Simply remove the agitator of your washing machine, add greens, and set it on the spin cycle. Don't load too much at a time, or leaves will become crushed and bruised.

Today, most information on foraging legalities can be found on the internet or by calling local officials. Try to determine the agency in charge of the public property, whether a school district, parks department, street rights-of-way, or university campus. You might have to contact city, county, school, or even state agencies in order to make sure your foraging is permitted.

BE ENVIRONMENTALLY RESPONSIBLE

Finding and harvesting your own food can be a very rewarding way to interact with nature. But even with plants we call weeds, there is potential for carelessness and abuse.

Fill your holes, pack up and take your garbage, do what you can to limit damage to surrounding plant life, and don't harvest a plant if there are just a few around. Leave several leaves on each weed you harvest from so the plant can sustain itself and produce new growth. Consider the resiliency of the species you're harvesting from. If it's a hardy perennial like dandelion, cat's ear, or plantain, you can do some pretty heavy harvesting with no ill result. If it's a tender annual, treat the plant more gently.

Before you harvest from a weed patch, ask yourself what type of impacts your activities might leave behind, then mitigate them. Are these plants being foraged by animals or other people? Will your harvest leave a visual impact? What quantity can you harvest without harming the continuation of the species in the surrounding area? Are you harvesting more than you can use or store? Are there more abundant sources nearby?

With a little common sense, you can find plenty to forage without negatively impacting the environment.

Foraging Tips

Urban foraging doesn't have to be complicated or require a lot of planning, but here are a few suggestions to make it easier to enjoy spontaneous weed-gathering forays.

WHAT TOOLS TO BRING

I often forage for urban weeds with nothing more than my bare hands since it's easiest and I'm not too worried about hardy weeds becoming diseased because I didn't use sterilized scissors. However, depending on what you're foraging for, bring along the following to make your gathering easier:

- Clean scissors: to cut stems
- Trowel and/or shovel: to dig roots
- Cloth or paper bags: to separate different kinds of plants or different parts of a plant
- Basket(s): to contain multiple bags
- Camera: to record a gathering location
- Plant identification book(s): to ensure positive plant identification

WHAT TO WEAR

You can forage spontaneously whenever you make a good find, but depending on the season or surroundings, your foray will be more comfortable if you wear the following:

- Gloves: cloth gardening gloves or heavier leather gloves for thorny plants
- Long-sleeved shirt: arm protection from sun and prickly plants
- Heavy denim clothing: heavier protection for bigger jobs
- Weather-appropriate attire: raingear, sun protection, cold-weather clothing, etc.
- Boots: soles with good traction, high-cut for ankle support or protection, water resistant or waterproof.

How to Enjoy Your New Adventure

Be willing to explore new flavors and textures. We have all developed tastes for foods we initially abhorred, such as beer, coffee, or broccoli. But very often, strongly flavored plants contain high concentrations of healthful phytochemicals and antioxidants. Many such foods are worth the learning curve; some of Earth's most nutrient-packed plants have bitter or tart flavors. If you aspire to be a good forager, you must be at least a little bit adventuresome!

How to Use This Book

This book includes the 30 most common and useful urban weeds, from ones that we all know and recognize, like dandelions, to those you might be less familiar with even though they're all around you. I describe how to find them, identify them, and cook with them. Each chapter covers a type of location where urban foraging can be productive, from your own yard and garden to parks and vacant lots. Within each chapter, plants are listed in alphabetical order by their most widely recognized common name; other common names and the plant's scientific name are also provided. Depending on the sources you use for plant identification, you might find variances in what a plant is called, but usually the scientific name is definitive (see Know What to Call It, above).

Each plant's listing is divided into two sections: **In the Field** includes a comprehensive physical description of the plant, the locations where it's found, the best times to harvest it, the edible parts of the plant, harvesting methods, and poisonous look-alikes to avoid. **In the Kitchen** includes the plant's nutritional value, other concerns about edibility, flavor notes, storage methods, and cooking tips as well as recipes to enable you to bring the plant to your table in delicious—and sometimes unexpected—ways. (A list of all the recipes in this book is given at the beginning of this book.)

At the end of the book you'll find a list of poisonous plants (also listed alphabetically) commonly found in urban areas, a glossary, and recommended resources. If you can't take this book along with you in the field, take a notebook to record your harvests and help you keep track of plants you've identified and gathered as well as your favorite locales. Happy foraging!

Getting kids involved

Children have an amazing aptitude for recognizing edible plants. Enlisting their help in foraging not only offers a fun activity for you to do together but can be truly helpful in bringing dinner to the table.

Start with the obvious: teach your children one plant at a time. Focus on plant features your child can easily identify. For example, point out how almost all clover leaves feature a white circle near the center of their triplet leaves. Spend a relaxing afternoon picking clover from the front yard and then make a simple cream of clover soup (see recipes).

Try not to micromanage. Once you've taught your child a plant, let her independently identify what to pick until she's filled her gathering container. Together you can remove any unwanted material once you're back in the kitchen. Very soon, both you and your children will feel confident about their ability to discern plants from one another.

Invite your child's assistance in setting the menu. Often, children come up with unique and creative ways to cook with foraged foods. For example, my niece thought it would be fun to add clover flowers to her bowl of Lucky Charms cereal. Let children create their own green smoothie recipes with weeds they've collected from the yard. This works well for pesto recipes too. See the recipes in this book.

Give your children their own plant identification book. A wonderful children's nature guide series called *Take Along Guides* by Diane Burns includes the books *Berries, Nuts and Seeds* and *Wildflowers, Blooms and Blossoms*. Of course, your children should avoid trying to learn plants with poisonous look-alikes until they are at least 12 years of age.

Nancy Ross Hugo, author of *Seeing Trees: Discover the Extraordinary Secrets of Everyday Trees,* suggests holding a contest to find the smallest and the largest leaves from a particular kind of tree. Suzanne Mackey of Petaluma Urban Homestead says to have kids start with edible flowers, which have so much color and are easy to identify. Then move on to the greens. She finds that once kids are turned on to the greens, you will never stop hearing, "Can I eat that?"

Encourage your children to collect seeds of plants they enjoy eating. Then give them a small plot or a planter in which to sow their own weed garden.

Give your children a nature journal in which to record drawings, descriptions, and locations of wild food sources they've discovered. Also, give your children their own blank cookbook so they can record the foraging recipes they like and those they've invented.

Above all, make urban foraging a fun activity rather than a chore. For children, foraging is generally more fun when done with another person—and not for so long a period that it becomes a turnoff.

*One must ask children
and birds how cherries and
strawberries taste.*

—Johann Wolfgang von Goethe

2 | LAWNS AND PARKING STRIPS

Looking for the Garden of Eden? Look down! Many if not most of the plants right at your feet are edible. Yes, even the grass and clover and especially the dandelions and cat's ear.

On learning about some of my early lawn foraging exploits, my brother Jim, the comedian in the family, told me he'd raked up his autumn leaves for a delicious fall-flavored brown smoothie. Very funny.

Later, when I told him most of his lawn was edible, he sent me a drawing of his "patent-pending lawnmower cum salad shooter." His drawing showed an ample salad bowl where the grass catcher would normally be. While my brother's "invention" is not an entirely bad idea, I doubt I'll go that far. After all, I do have *some* standards.

This chapter will help you to define your own standards for deciding which lawn weeds are suitable for your table. After eating from your lawn, I guarantee that you'll never look at it in the same way again.

Note that while these weeds are common to your front yard "green-carpet," they grow in many other urban spaces too.

Cat's Ear

Flatweed, False or Coast Dandelion, Gosmore
Hypochaeris radicata

Anything with a yellow ray flower sprouting from a clump of low-lying serrated leaves is some type of dandelion, right? This is how I long categorized yellow flowers growing in my lawn. For many years, I thought cat's ear was just an informed dandelion, a plant that had learned to crouch just beneath the grass to avoid the ruthless blade of my mower. But once I began researching edible weeds, I learned that, while indeed it has "learned" to grow low in lawns and closely resembles the dandelion, cat's ear is in fact its own species. I'm happy to say that this becomes especially clear once you've taken a bite of it, for cat's ear is almost never bitter like dandelion leaves can be.

Cat's ear is a perennial, low-lying herb very common in (wonderfully) unkempt lawns. It is native to Europe but is now also at home in Japan, Australia, New Zealand, and the Americas, where it is often considered an invasive weed. The common name refers to the plant leaves' fuzzy, softly rounded tips. The genus name *Hypochaeris* comes from the Greek for "young pig," possibly because pigs are said to enjoy its long, fleshy roots.

Though Seattle is best known for its rain, our summers are very dry. By the end of July, unwatered lawns are a light tan with occasional islands of green. Those islands are usually cat's ear plants. With its long, fibrous taproot, cat's ear is very drought tolerant and quite at home in poor soils.

For me, this raises the question, why not lawns of 100 percent cat's ear? It grows in poor soils, is frost hardy, enjoys being walked on, doesn't grow tall enough to require mowing, is drought tolerant and, have I mentioned, is edible! Believe it or not, there is a partial answer to this question. Athletes and golfers are not in favor of cat's ear because it can be slippery when wet, potentially even more slippery than grass.

In spite of this complaint, I advocate for lawns of cat's ear and other edible weeds, omitting the grass altogether. (I can hear the environmentalists' response now: "Yeah, but they're not native and you'd be helping a weed proliferate! Bad advice!" Well, lawn grasses aren't native either, yet here we are.)

Cat's ear is thought to be as nutritious as dandelion and less bitter, and it has a longer growing season. In many climates, you can harvest its leaves year-round. In Europe, especially in Sicily and Crete, cat's ear is still commonly served with olive oil and garlic. Beyond its food value, cat's ear's medicinal properties are considered to be similar to dandelion. Because of its nutrient content and productivity, cat's ear is considered a valuable grassland plant. Sheep, pigs, and some wildlife often prefer the plant over more traditional pasture species.

Any way you look at it (unless you're a golfer), cat's ear is superior to grass in a lawn. I think planting it in the lawn is such a great idea I'm considering starting a seed-selling business specializing in cat's ear and other edible weeds. (I will undoubtedly bump up against a few hurdles: It turns out most states have at least some prohibitions on selling seeds of invasive or pest species, whether they're edible or not).

IN THE FIELD

What It Looks Like: Leaves grow up to 8 inches long, occasionally longer, lobed, covered in fine hairs on both sides. Typically, leaves form a flat basal rosette, though in rich, moist, shaded soils they can present themselves as upright. Stiff, wiry, solid, hairless, leafless, branching stems 8–16 inches tall usually carry multiple ¾- to 1½-inch-diameter yellow flower heads. Blooms from early spring through September. When mature, flower heads form seeds attached to windborne "parachutes" similar to those of dandelions. Plants produce, on average, 20 flower heads during a single season, with 40 or more seeds in each head. Plant capable of growing rapidly, going from seed to maturity within a couple of months. Cat's ear can also reproduce vegetatively: new plants form from buds that are dislodged by humans or animals. Thus, if you walk on your lawn, there's a good chance you are helping your cat's ear multiply.

Where to Find: Occurs throughout the United States, except for Arizona, Iowa, Kansas, Minnesota, Nebraska, North Dakota, Oklahoma, and South Dakota. Common in lawns, golf courses, pastures, roadsides, gardens, disturbed areas, waste areas.

When to Harvest: In milder climates, year-round; elsewhere, spring, summer, fall. Not frost tender; hardy to –20°F. Leaves tenderest before plant flowers.

What to Eat: All parts are edible; however, leaves and roots are most often harvested.

How to Harvest: Cut or tear leaves at the base. Leave a couple leaves behind so the plant can easily grow back. When harvesting flowers, take entire stem so plant can redirect its energy to roots and remaining leaves.

Poisonous Look-Alikes to Avoid: None.

IN THE KITCHEN

Why You Should Eat It: Similar to dandelion; rich source of vitamins and minerals. Said to have many medicinal properties; used by herbalists to treat liver, kidney, and gallbladder problems as well rheumatoid arthritis.

Who Should Avoid It: People on potassium-sparing diuretics, since its high potassium content can lead to hyperkalemia.

What It Tastes Like: Leaves and flowers have little flavor and, in contrast to dandelion, only rarely exhibit bitterness. Roots are somewhat bitter, but less so than dandelion roots.

How to Store: Like lettuce, store leaves in a loose plastic bag in refrigerator's vegetable crisper drawer. (See Storing Urban Weeds sidebar in chapter 1 for more options.)

How to Cook: Similar uses as dandelion. In Crete and other parts of Greece, leaves are eaten raw in salads, boiled, or steamed as any other leafy vegetable. Roast the root and grind it to form a coffee substitute. Batter the flowers and make into fritters as well as add to other dishes as a flavoring.

Cat's ear has composite flowers with each flower resembling a petal. Note that each cat's ear flower has 5 notches at its tip.

Cat's Ear Fusion Quesadilla

The name cat's ear offers no appetizing ring whatsoever. Nor do flatweed or false dandelion or, for that matter, Hypochaeris radicata. *I hope that by using the word "fusion" in the title (Greek-meets-Mexican fusion), a word so often used on trendy menus, I will ignite enough gustatory curiosity to entice you to try this simple but delicious recipe.*

* MAKES 4 QUESADILLAS *

5 cups cat's ear leaves, coarsely chopped
2 tablespoons extra virgin olive oil
8 corn tortillas
8 ounces cheddar, shredded
2 tablespoons canned jalapeño chiles, minced
½ teaspoon ground cumin

Steam cat's ear until tender, about 3–5 minutes. Set aside.

Heat a bit of olive oil in a large skillet or griddle over medium-high heat. Lay a tortilla on the hot skillet. Sprinkle with shredded cheese. Cover with a layer of cat's ear. Sprinkle with a small amount of jalapeños and cumin. Sprinkle with another layer of shredded cheese. Place a second tortilla on top and press down with back of spatula.

Cook for 1–2 minutes, then carefully turn it over. Press down again with the spatula. Cook until cheese melts and tortillas are golden. If you're in a rush you can get a similar result using a microwave. Serve halved or quartered.

Cat's Ear and Clam Linguine

I've made this linguine with many of the plants described in this book, but I think cat's ear works the best because the leaves retain their hearty texture even after they're boiled, so they do not disappear into the mixture as some other greens do. And because they're so mildly flavored, they easily absorb the clam, wine, and butter flavors, adding a very healthy green to a classic dish.

* SERVES 4 *

1 pound linguine
¼ cup butter
4 cloves garlic, minced
2 shallots, coarsely chopped
½ teaspoon crushed red pepper flakes
3 tablespoons good salami, diced
2 pounds small fresh clams, scrubbed
⅔ cup dry white wine
2 cups cat's ear leaves, chopped to 1-inch pieces
Sea salt and freshly ground pepper to taste

Cook the linguine in boiling water until it's al dente and set aside.

While the pasta is cooking, in a large skillet over medium heat, sauté in butter the garlic, shallots, red pepper flakes, and salami until shallots are softened. Add clams and wine and bring to a simmer. Cover the pan and simmer until the clams open, about 5 minutes.

Add the cat's ear and al dente pasta. Cook on medium heat until the pasta has absorbed almost all of the remaining liquid. Add salt and pepper to taste. Serve immediately.

Eating grass

With more than 10,000 species of grasses, the Poaceae family, also known as the Gramineae family, is the fifth largest in the plant kingdom. Many seasoned foragers will tell you that none of these species are poisonous. However, there may be a few exceptions within the hybridized ornamental grasses. And though it's not toxic per se, reed canary grass exhibits hallucinogenic properties due to its concentrations of LSA, a chemical similar to LSD.

Of course, we're all familiar with eating the cereal grains that come from grasses: wheat, rye, barley, rice, etc. But most of us learned at an early age that only cows and other ruminants are able to digest the green or blade portion of grasses. The bacteria housed in their multiple stomachs are able to transform cellulose fiber into proteins and fats. Our own digestive systems, however, lack such sophisticated fermentation vats, thus cellulose is simply excreted from our bodies, as is any other type of fiber.

We certainly already eat a lot of cellulose, most of it coming from wood pulp. Many processed foods from crackers and ice creams to puddings and baked goods contain cellulose as a food extender. In the food industry, adding cellulose is seen as boosting fiber intake, extending shelf life of various processed foods, and improving texture (its water absorbing properties make foods feel like they contain more fat). The FDA has declared it safe for human consumption. (Ordinarily, I don't listen much to the FDA, but in this case, common sense tells me they are right.) The FDA sets no limit on the amount of cellulose that can be used in our foods except in the case of meat, which can contain no more than 3.5 percent cellulose.

In the early 1990s, my athletic club started selling wheat grass juice. At first I mused that surely those flats of bright green stuff were something other than actual "grass." But eventually I learned it really is what it says it is: wheat grass is nothing more than the seedlings of wheat berries—the same plant we sow to grow wheat!

To each his own, I thought; weirdo hippy freaks. It took a long time before I'd even taste the stuff. One day, one of the smiling, perky trainers stood near the front door handing out samples in small paper cups. When she shoved the cup into my hand, peer pressure kicked in and I felt I had no choice but to at least give it a try. I knocked back my shot. It tasted like, well, grass! And you know what? Grass really isn't so bad! One thing is for sure: it gave my workout a heck of a kick.

Humans don't digest cellulose well, but we do get some caloric content from it, and because it's hydrophilic, it acts as a bulking fiber to aid elimination. Our bodies can also make excellent use of grass's robust concentrations of vitamins, minerals, and phytochemicals. And not only does the act of juicing remove that pesky pulp, but it makes the nutritional punch that much more available to our bodies.

Don't have a juicer and you're looking for some emergency food? Grab a handful of your lawn, chew it, swallow the juice, and spit out the fibrous pulp. You won't get enough calories to sustain yourself on grass, but at least you'll be getting some of your daily nutritional allowances, and then some.

While I recommend it, you really don't even need to spit out the pulp. Cellulose may not be very digestible, but it's not in the least bit toxic to us. It's just that, as with other high-fiber foods, you should build up from small amounts or risk the same kind of gastrointestinal stress you might experience after eating a couple of cans of refried beans. To add nutrition to your foods, grass can even be cut finely and cooked in breads and soups, or steeped as tea.

I know this all sounds really weird, and it's not likely that I will make a daily habit of it. But odd as it seems, humans have already been eating grasses for a very long time—bamboo shoots, sugar cane, and lemon grass are all in the Poaceae family.

So you see, as whack as it sounds, even eating the *grass* in your front lawn can be very beneficial to your health. And incredibly convenient and inexpensive!

All wild grass seeds are also edible, though some are more nutritious and flavorful than others. In addition to being used as flour, all grass seeds make good cooked cereals and additions to granola.

Most grasses have tiny seeds, so grinding them loosely and then letting the wind or a fan blow most of the chaff from the seeds is the easiest way to process them. The chaff will not hurt you if it's ground finely; it is simply not always digestible and much of it will pass out unchanged.

CAUTION: Stored grain is a good medium for

Lawn grass: the next health food fad? *(Photo by Leon Brooks)*

molds and fungi, some of which are poisonous to humans. For example, the fungus ergot infects rye cereal, and some scientists believe the resulting convulsions, hallucinations, and delirium were the basis for the Salem witch trials. Also, once ground, grain oils become rancid and unhealthy over time. It's best to store grains whole and grind them just prior to use.

Chickweed

Nodding Chickweed, Stitchwort, Starwort, White Bird's Eye, Tongue Grass
Stellaria media

The first time I tried eating chickweed, I found it so disgusting I spat it out immediately. A couple years later I tried it again and loved it! Why the difference? I suspect the terroir (the local soil's expression through the plant) is especially noticeable in some of the more watery or succulent greens such as chickweed, miner's lettuce, and purslane. I don't recall where my first bite came from, but the second handful I tried came from Seattle Tilth's garden, a plot of soil that had undergone years of sweetening via good organic gardening practices and it was delicately scrumptious. Nowadays, I seem to find the tastiest chickweed in moist, partially shaded areas.

Common chickweed is a somewhat succulent herbaceous annual plant that, given enough space, often forms dense sprawling mounds. Aptly named, it's not only loved by people but has a spot high on the typical chicken's list of treats. Chickweed is believed to have originated in Eurasia, but it is now cosmopolitan, occurring even in the Arctic and Antarctic and from sea level up to 15,000 feet. The botanical name *Stellaria media* means "little star in the midst."

Besides being tasty, chickweed can be used as a barometer to predict rain. If you see the blossoms wide open, you probably have at least three hours before it rains again; if the blossoms are closed, take an umbrella. Regardless of weather patterns, the blossoms seem to enjoy sleeping in, opening late in the morning even on the sunniest day.

Chickweed has a long history of human use. It's been found in preneolithic archaeological digs in Great Britain, and its use as a medicinal plant can be traced back to at least the 16th century when it was used to sooth inflammations, skin conditions, and numerous other diseases. Even today its popularity as a health remedy is reflected in natural food stores where chickweed is found in capsules, liquid extracts, dried herb, oils, tea bags, ointments, and tinctures.

IN THE FIELD

What It Looks Like: Plants usually run flat along the ground, rooting at the nodes, with upper portion erect and freely branching. Stems light green with single hairs in vertical rows that change sides with each pair of leaves. Leaves oval or elliptic, light green, smooth, ½–1 inch long, and arranged oppositely. Upper leaves lack stems (petioles); those of lower leaves are long. Flowers borne alone or in small clusters at ends of stems. Flowers small (⅛–¼ inch wide) and white, consisting of five deeply lobed petals (giving the appearance of 10 petals). Roots shallow and fibrous. Plant does not exude milky sap.

Where to Find: Widespread throughout North America; occurs throughout the United States. Prefers cool and damp conditions; will not survive where it's dry and hot.

When to Harvest: Germinates in winter; best eaten in spring and fall.

What to Eat: Entire plant.

How to Harvest: Palm up, slide your fingers into the lower portion of the foliage mat. Using your fingers like a comb, loosely pull up along the stems until the leaves are bunched in your hand. Hold the lower stems with the other hand as you gently pull upward to pluck the upper leaves off.

Poisonous Look-Alikes to Avoid: Scarlet pimpernel (*Anagallis arvensis*) has similar features and, if eaten in quantity, can cause mild illness. However, it's easy to distinguish the two because chickweed flowers are white whereas scarlet pimpernel flowers are orange to red. See chapter 6, Poisonous Weeds Common to Urban Areas.

IN THE KITCHEN

Why You Should Eat It: High in vitamin C, vitamin A, calcium, magnesium, niacin, potassium, riboflavin, selenium, thiamin, zinc, copper, and gamma-linolenic acid. Contains chromium, copper, manganese, iron, and silicon. In addition, contains respectable levels of B complex vitamins.

What It Tastes Like: A favorite salad green, it's often described as tasting like corn silk when raw. Once cooked, it takes on the flavor of spinach, though the texture is its own.

How to Store: Store in a loose plastic bag in refrigerator's vegetable crisper drawer, where it will keep for up to a week. (See Storing Urban Weeds sidebar in chapter 1 for more options.)

How to Cook: Use in salads and sandwiches and as a garnish. Also add to soups or stews at the last minute so as not to overcook.

Chickweed flowers are tiny and have 5 deeply notched petals.

Chickweed "Sprouts" with Goat Cheese in Toasted Veggie Sandwiches

Never have I met a weed that more closely resembles alfalfa sprouts in a sandwich, and chickweed's mild flavor makes it an obvious substitution. I consider it an improvement over store-bought alfalfa sprouts because it has a nuttier flavor, I can pick it absolutely fresh, and I know exactly from which corner of my organic yard it came.

❋ MAKES 4 HALF SANDWICHES ❋

2 tablespoons mayonnaise, divided
1 teaspoon balsamic vinegar
1 teaspoon honey
1 cup chickweed, rinsed and patted dry
4 slices of bread (use your favorite)
1 tablespoon Dijon mustard
½ ripe avocado, sliced lengthwise ¼ inch thick
1 roasted red pepper, sliced lengthwise ½ inch thick
2 slices hard chévre or 2 tablespoons soft chévre
6 kalamata olives, pitted and minced
Salt and pepper to taste

Blend 1 tablespoon mayonnaise with vinegar and honey. Add chickweed and toss.

Toast bread. For each sandwich, spread a slice of bread with Dijon mustard and another slice with remaining mayonnaise. Layer avocado, red peppers, cheese, dressed chickweed, and kalamata olives between the two pieces of toast. Season to taste. Slice in half diagonally and serve.

Chickweed Falafel Pita Pockets

While you can certainly improve upon this recipe by making your own homemade falafel, yogurt, and pita pockets, there is nothing fundamentally wrong with seeking convenience, and so this recipe uses a prepared falafel mix as well as store-bought pita pockets and yogurt. Don't be afraid to tinker with this recipe. Consider incorporating other strong flavors you enjoy, such as kalamata olives, sun-dried tomatoes, or additional cilantro.

✳ MAKES 4 PITA POCKETS ✳

2 large, whole pita pockets
4–6 prepared falafel patties (prepare dried mix per instructions)
1 cup diced cucumber
2 cups chickweed, loosely packed
1 tomato, diced

YOGURT SAUCE
1 cup plain Greek yogurt
1 teaspoon lemon zest
1 tablespoon freshly squeezed lemon juice
½ teaspoon salt
2 tablespoons coarsely chopped parsley or cilantro leaves
1 teaspoon ground cumin

Slice the two pita breads in half to make four pockets. Tuck into each half pita pocket one or two falafel patties, ¼ cup diced cucumber, and ½ cup chickweed.

Whisk together all the yogurt sauce ingredients and drizzle one-fourth over each pita's contents. Alternatively, serve the yogurt sauce in a separate bowl for dipping.

Chickweed is highly nutritious, low in calories, and delicious.

Nuts, grains, fruit, and fish,
to regale ev'ry palate,
And groundsel and chickweed
serv'd up in a salad.

—Catherine Ann Turner,
The Peacock "At Home"

Clover

White Clover, Sweet Clover, Shamrock, Trifoil
Trifolium repens

n the early '70s I played barefoot in a backyard full of white clover, which made our yard smell sweet; we used to pick the little white petals to suck nectar from their bases. Back then, we had to carefully watch where we stepped as there seemed to be a honeybee or bumblebee on nearly every flower. While stepping around bees one summer, my brother found a four-leaf clover, which launched a summer-long project of looking for more. Over the course of the season, I think we found about 20 four-leaf clovers in that same plot of grass. Call me superstitious, but since that time, we have both been extraordinarily lucky in life.

Clovers can also have five, six, or more leaves, but these are even more uncommon than the rare four-leafed version. (*Guinness Book of World Records* lists the most leaves ever observed on a single clover as 56.)

White clover is an herbaceous perennial native to Europe and Asia, introduced to the Americas by colonists. It's commonly fed to livestock and, as a nitrogen fixer, used by farmers to improve soil. Clover flowers are an important source of nectar for bees and other pollinating insects. (Our honeybees were also imported from Europe, where the two species evolved together.) Beekeepers often grow white clover to produce the popular mildly flavored clover honey.

For a long time, I thought shamrocks were the plant oxalis because that's what florists sell on St. Patrick's Day, but the real shamrock is white clover. The word "shamrock" is derived from the Irish word for clover, *seamróg.* The word "clover" is thought to probably be from the German *klaiwaz,* or "sticky pap," owing to a type of honey made from white clover nectar. The genus name *Trifolium* means "three leaves" and the species name *repens* means "creeping or crawling."

For millennia, white clover has been considered a good luck charm, and in medieval times people used it to ward off evil spirits. Plants with four leaves were considered especially lucky for farmers as they were thought to be an indication of good soil and potentially increased yields.

Some people, myself included, favor clover above grass in their lawns. It's a perennial, spreads quickly, tolerates and improves poor soils, is winter hardy, frost tolerant, and drought tolerant. It also emits a most heavenly scent when it's walked upon.

While all these are wonderful attributes, they distract from the source of one of clover's biggest bragging rights: the entire plant is edible and nutritious!

IN THE FIELD

What It Looks Like: Low-lying legume with underground stems (stolons) radiating from the crown and rooting at the nodes. Stems and compound trifoliate leaves hairless. Leaflets oval or heart-shaped and generally exhibit a pale chevron pattern on upper surface. Flower head round and pompom-like. Each pompom contains 30–40 white flowers that mature to small, brown, oblong seedpods. Most of the root system is within top 10 inches of soil, but roots can reach depths of 3 feet or more.

Where to Find: Occurs throughout the United States in a wide range of habitats, including dry meadows, mudflats, woods margins, open woods, banks of rivers and brooks, plains, semideserts, and mountains up to subalpine meadows. Frequently found in agricultural fields and pasture, in lawns and gardens, on roadsides, and in barren areas.

When to Harvest: Spring, summer, fall.

What to Eat: Leaves, flowers, seeds, roots.

How to Harvest: Harvest flowers and leaves from the base. No need to remove tender, edible young stems. Harvest roots year-round.

Poisonous Look-Alikes to Avoid: None.

IN THE KITCHEN

Why You Should Eat It: For a plant, it's high in protein. Also contains significant amounts of calcium, chromium, magnesium, niacin, phosphorus, potassium, thiamine, and vitamin C. Considered a dark green vegetable, clover has the same healthy nutritional qualities that spinach does. White clover infusions have been used medicinally for centuries, especially in response to respiratory complaints.

What It Tastes Like: Distinctly like . . . clover! Sweet!

How to Store: Dry or store in the refrigerator as you would store lettuce, for up to three days.

How to Cook: Eat young leaves, harvested before the plant flowers, raw in salads. As plant matures, cook the leaves. Dried leaves add a slightly vanilla-like flavor to baked goods. Use flowers raw in salads or sautéed or stir-fried. Raw flower heads and leaves easier to eat if soaked in water for an hour. Use dried flowers and seeds as a tea or ground into flour. Typically eat roots cooked.

CLOVER

*To make a prairie it takes
a clover and one bee,
One clover, and a bee,
And revery.
The revery alone will do,
If bees are few.*

—Emily Dickinson

Clover Chimichurri

When you serve your family and friends a helping of grass-fed beefsteaks, treat them to the image of the sweet-smelling meadow the cows grazed in by dressing the meat with a generous helping of this wonderful sauce. Clover chimichurri tastes clean and green against the heaviness of red meat. Background notes are exactly the flavor of standing in a lush field of clover, watching cows peacefully grazing.

* MAKES ABOUT 2 CUPS *

1 cup loosely packed fresh clover leaves and blossoms (stems and roots fine too), finely chopped

2 tablespoons fresh parsley, finely chopped

2 tablespoons cilantro, finely chopped

1 cayenne or jalapeño pepper, finely chopped

½ teaspoon crushed red chile flakes

½ teaspoon dried oregano

2 tablespoons capers, finely chopped

Juice of one lime

3 tablespoons red wine vinegar

5 cloves garlic, minced

⅛ cup extra virgin olive oil

Salt and pepper to taste

Blend all ingredients in a food processor. Let it sit for at least 30 minutes prior to using (to allow flavors to marry.) Serve on grilled steaks. Use within a day.

Clover Soup

Filling soups of creamed or pureed greens are among my favorite meals. This recipe is for those counting calories, but for a creamier, richer version, add a cup of milk or heavy cream. Either version elicits a quiet, satisfied "mmmm" with every sip.

* SERVES 8 *

2 shallots, chopped

2 cloves garlic, minced

3 tablespoons butter

2 cups white clover flowers and leaves (stems and roots fine too), coarsely chopped

4 cups chicken or vegetable broth

3 medium potatoes, peeled and quartered

Salt and pepper to taste

For an interesting and attractive hint of sweet, add whole clover heads to salad greens.

In a large saucepan over medium heat, sauté shallots and garlic in butter. When shallots are softened, add clover and stir to coat. Add broth and bring to a boil. Add potatoes and cook on medium heat until potatoes are soft, about 15 minutes. Drain and reserve the cooking broth.

Puree the drained clover mixture in a food processor. Blend the reserved cooking broth with the puree. Bring to a boil, then reduce heat and simmer for a couple minutes. Add salt and pepper to taste. Serve hot.

Dandelion

Common Dandelion, Pee-the-Bed, Lion's Teeth, Blowball, Wild Endive, Piss-a-Bed
Taraxacum officinale

One of my husband's college buddies, Bernard, is from the Virgin Islands. One day, shortly after they'd met, Bernard said, "I found this incredibly beautiful flower growing at the edge of a drainage ditch. I dug it up so you can tell me what it is." Carlos did not consider himself much of a botanist then but said he would make an attempt to identify it. When he entered Bernard's apartment, there on the coffee table was a flowerpot containing none other than a common dandelion. I hope I always see my front yard, filled with humble dandelions, through the eyes of our friend Bernard.

Common dandelion is an herbaceous perennial that is identified by most of us by its bright yellow flowers and round puffball seed heads. They are a highly successful plant for a number of reasons. Like other members of the aster family, their composite flowers are comprised of many individual flowers, or florets. Each composite can produce as many as 175 one-seeded fruits, and a single plant can produce as many as 5000 seeds per year. Dandelions tolerate many growing conditions and most soil types. Seeds will germinate without going through cold temperatures. Also, seeds remain viable for 10 or more years. Add to that, even the smallest bits of dandelion root are capable of generating new plants.

Taraxacum is a large genus of flowering plants in the family Asteraceae. They are native to Europe, Asia, and North America. *Taraxacum officinale* is now found worldwide. The name dandelion comes from the French *dent de lion* or "lion's tooth." *Taraxacum officinale* has had many English common names, including blowball, cankerwort, milk witch, Irish daisy, monks head, priest's crown, puffball, faceclock, and piss-the-bed (it's an effective diuretic).

Dandelion has been used as a potherb and medicinal plant throughout Europe since Roman times. Explorers and immigrants alike brought common dandelion to North America for use as food and medicine. The entire plant is edible, a powerhouse of dense nutrition comparable to superfoods such as spinach and kale.

In spite of its history as a useful plant, in our day the dandelion has become suburbia's worst enemy. Not only is it a pest for the perfectly manicured lawn, but it's also considered a problem for athletic fields and golf courses—for aesthetic reasons, but also because it can result in a slippery surface for athletes. Homeowners, athletic fields, and golf courses spend billions of dollars each year on herbicides designed to eradicate dandelion.

But even with this significant negative shift in our culture's perception of dandelion, it is still considered food or beverage to many. Here in the United States, you can still find cellars with bottles of homemade dandelion wine, for which there are many recipes. Belgians continue to make an ale they call Pissenlit (French for "wet the bed.") It's still fairly common knowledge that dried, ground dandelion root makes a respectable coffee substitute (see Dandelion Coffee from Roasted Roots). Many folks love the unique flavor of dandelion flower jam. And as a leafy green, it has never fallen out of favor in many parts of Europe.

Recently, a few farmers in the United States have begun growing dandelion as a commercial leaf vegetable and selling it at a premium price. The leafy greens are most often found in specialty stores and farmers markets, but I've also occasionally seen it in large chain stores. You know you are in a fine restaurant if your entrée comes with a side of dandelion greens. To think these same delicacies can be had for free from your own front yard!

In addition to its food and medicine value, the dandelion's milky latex has been used as a mosquito repellent and wart remover.

IN THE FIELD

What It Looks Like: Long, lance-shaped leaves often deeply serrated (forming a "lion's tooth" outline), generally 3–14 inches long, ½–3 inches wide. Leaves grow from a basal rosette. Plants bear one to more than ten hollow stems, typically 2–24 inches tall, upright or prone, each producing a single flower head held as tall or taller than the leaves. Each yellow corolla contains 100–300 yellow ray flowers, or florets. Achenes (seedpods) about ⅛ inch in length, range in color from olive-green to grayish, have six to eight parallel ribs. When flowers fruit or go to seed, they form a ball of silky parachutes, or pappi, is white to silver-white, 2–3 inches in diameter. These pappi allow seeds to be transported for miles by wind. Flowers not normally pollinated but develop asexually. Roots are almost always unbranched taproots that commonly penetrate soil to depths of 6–18 inches, occasionally up to 10–15 feet. When a plant is severed from its root, it produces a crown of buds that can regenerate new plants. Even small sections of root are capable of producing new plants. Plants can survive for many years, developing massive, thickened crowns 6–10 inches across. Stems and larger, older leaves exude a milky sap when severed.

Where to Find: Occurs in all 50 of the United States and most Canadian provinces. Especially suited to disturbed areas such as lawns and sunny, open places. Grows best in moist areas in full sun, but once established can survive shade and droughty conditions.

When to Harvest: Year-round in mild climates. Blooms from March until October. Roots are most nutrient dense in late fall to early spring.

What to Eat: Entire plant.

How to Harvest: To remove a root, wait for a heavy rain, then dig several inches deep all around the plant. Gather all the leaves and stems in your hand as close to the ground as possible; to prevent roots from breaking, slowly pull the plant straight up. For easier cleaning, soak roots for 10–15 minutes before scrubbing them. To collect flowers, remove

Dandelion flowers lie waiting to become delicious fritters.

entire stem from plant. When collecting leaves, be sure to leave one or two leaves behind so plant can more easily regenerate.

Poisonous Look-Alikes to Avoid: None.

IN THE KITCHEN

Why You Should Eat It: Leaves rich in potassium, antioxidants, vitamin A, vitamin D, iron, and zinc and contain more iron and calcium than spinach. Affects the digestive system by acting as a mild laxative, increasing appetite, and improving digestion. Has been used to treat liver problems, kidney disease, inflammation, high cholesterol, skin problems, eye problems, fever, diabetes, diarrhea, heartburn, and upset stomach. Dandelion root is a registered drug in Canada, sold principally as a diuretic. A hepatoprotective effect of chemicals extracted from dandelion root has been reported, and the plant is known for its ability to treat jaundice, cholecystitis, and cirrhosis.

Who Should Avoid It: Generally considered safe; however, there have been a few reports of upset stomach and diarrhea, especially after use of concentrated dandelion (tinctures, powders, etc.). If you are allergic to ragweed, chrysanthemums, marigold, chamomile, yarrow, daisies, or iodine, you should avoid dandelion. People with kidney problems, gallbladder problems, or gallstones should ask their health care provider before eating dandelion.

What It Tastes Like: Raw leaves have a slightly bitter flavor. Leaves are least bitter before the plant flowers. You can remove much or all of the bitterness by removing the center midrib of each leaf. Though this sounds labor intensive, using your fingers to gently "squeegee" the leaves from the stem makes the work go quickly. You can actually pick the leaves this way, leaving the midrib behind. The cooked greens taste very much like spinach. If you do get a bitter batch, sprinkle each serving with balsamic vinegar and you won't even notice it. Greens can also be cooked in two or three changes of water to remove most bitterness from older plants. I never do this because I don't want to lose all the nutrients into the water.

How to Store: Fresh-picked dandelion greens wilt quickly; clean in cold water and dry (a salad spinner is perfect). If you plan to use the dandelions within a day, store fresh leaves in a water glass with the leaf bases in an inch of water to help them retain their turgidity. Dry leaves, flowers, and roots and store in airtight containers. Blanch and freeze leaves.

How to Cook: Eat greens raw, steamed, boiled, sautéed, or braised. Harvest greens to be used raw before the first flower emerges. Larger greens tend to be tougher and more bitter and are said to be better suited for cooking. If you remove the midrib, even the older leaves can be delicious additions to salads. Eat the crowns and flowers raw or cooked. Roast the roots and brew like coffee or tea.

Dandelion coffee from roasted roots

Slice cleaned dandelion roots into thin, 2-inch-long pieces. If you are using a food dehydrator, arrange root pieces on its rack and dry for approximately one hour. If you don't have a food dehydrator, arrange the root slices on a baking sheet and place in a 200°F oven for 2 to 3 hours or until mostly dry and brittle to the touch, turning them a couple times throughout the process.

Remove the dandelion root slices from the dehydrator or oven. Chop the roots roughly into small, thumbnail-size pieces and arrange them on a baking sheet. There is no need to use a nonstick spray or oil. Roast at 400°F for 30 minutes, or until dry, brittle, and brown on all sides. Cool to room temperature.

Store the mix in an airtight container and use it for coffee, herbal medicine, and cooking. If using for coffee, grind just before use.

Dandelion Flower Fritters

These are very simple, fun, and quick to make, and my family and I just love eating them. The texture is soft and juicy but not mushy. Each bite carries a hint of flower without a trace of bitterness. Like anything frittered, the bright yellow flower heads are simply dipped in a light batter and fried in oil. Each batch of dandelions tend to bloom all at once, so we often eat these fritters several nights in a row to take advantage of their yellow deliciousness before they all go to seed. By the way, dandelion's signature shade of yellow is preserved through the cooking process, producing a lovely, appetizing dish. For a tasty alternative, cook them in unsalted butter.

* SERVES 4 *

About 20 fully opened dandelion flowers
½ cup white flour
½ cup rice flour
1 egg
1 cup milk
¼ teaspoon salt
¼ teaspoon garlic powder
¼ cup olive oil

Remove stems from flowers and discard stems; set flowers aside.

Whisk together flours, egg, milk, and seasonings.

Heat olive oil in a nonstick or cast-iron frying pan on medium high. Gently dip each flower into the batter to coat all sides. Place battered flowers face down in frying pan. Cook each side 3–4 minutes, until lightly browned. Remove to a paper towel to absorb excess oil; serve hot.

Dandelion Bourekas

Okay, to be perfectly honest, I'd never even heard of a boureka *until I began scouting out recipes for dandelion greens. Mouthwatering bourekas, where have you been all my life? Thought to have originated in the Ottoman Empire, bourekas (also called* borek *or* burek) *have long been a popular cuisine in North Africa and the Middle East. In the United States, they are most often prepared as part of a traditional Jewish meal. Dandelion greens are but one of many variations of boureka fillings—a scrumptious one at that.*

* MAKES 4 BOUREKAS *

2 tablespoons olive oil
1 bunch scallions, chopped
2 cloves garlic, minced
½ pound dandelion greens, rinsed,
**   midribs removed**
2 eggs lightly beaten, divided
½ cup goat or other feta cheese, crumbled
¼ cup Parmesan cheese, grated
1 10-by-15-inch sheet frozen puff pastry
2 tablespoons sesame seeds

Preheat oven to 375°F. Lightly oil a 28-by-18-inch baking sheet.

Heat olive oil in a large skillet over medium heat. Sauté scallions and garlic until soft and lightly browned. Stir in dandelion greens and sauté until greens are limp, about 2 minutes. Remove from heat and set aside to cool.

In a medium bowl, mix together half the egg mixture with feta and Parmesan. Combine with the dandelion mixture.

(Recipe continues on page 49.)

CLOCKWISE FROM TOP Both amaranth flower clusters (above) and seed heads (above, right) have a fluffy appearance. For the best bedstraw, pick it when it's young and under six inches tall.

CLOCKWISE FROM TOP LEFT When cat's ear flowers close up for the night, their darkly outlined bracts are very apparent. With cat's ear at your feet and pasta in the pantry, Cat's Ear Linguine is a simple, healthy meal. Chickweed forms low, dense mounds of tender greens.

CLOCKWISE FROM TOP LEFT White clover is common and easy to harvest for soup. Creeping wood sorrel comes in two varieties, purple and green; this example is bright green, but cross-pollination generates many shades in between. Dandelion roots can survive for years under pavement, lying in wait to penetrate the smallest crack. Dandelion Fritters are delicious, healthy, and fun to serve to guests.

CLOCKWISE FROM TOP LEFT All parts of the daylily are edible, not just the flower. Dead Nettle Crisps add a delicate, flavorful spike to any otherwise humdrum dish. Dead nettle is a creeping groundcover with larger leaves of green below diminishing to leaves of purple farther up; all leaves are distinctly hairy.

CLOCKWISE FROM TOP Dock leaves taste best before plants flower. In late summer dock bears towering clusters of rust- to brick-colored seeds; each seed is within a 3-sided achene. Dock Pesto is fabulous with oysters.

CLOCKWISE FROM TOP LEFT All parts of evening primrose are edible; pale yellow blooms continue from late spring through late summer. Lunaria is likely called 'honesty' due to its translucent seed pods. Honesty offers a lovely fragrance in the flower garden, especially in the evening.

CLOCKWISE FROM TOP The flowers of honesty are a lightly flavored, colorful addition to any salad. The horsetail shoot in the center of this photo is prime for harvesting; the stalk on the left has already become too coarse for consumption. Horsetail Shoots with Garlic, Butter, and Thyme.

CLOCKWISE FROM TOP Japanese knotweed often forms giant, impenetrable hedges. Lamb's-quarter leaves appear to wear a light dusting of ashes. Linden meal can be added to any recipe using flour, but expect the final result to take on a lovely shade of green.

CLOCKWISE FROM TOP A light green modified leaf shades the young fruits of the linden tree. Mallow fruits and seeds make great urban trail snacks. Young nipplewort leaves are choice and can be used with other salad greens.

CLOCKWISE FROM TOP Pineapple weed will happily sprout up through any crack in the sidewalk. Plantain is common in urban yards, gardens, and parks. Purslane is often found sprawling over pavement or concrete, but is erect if the conditions are right. *(Photo by Jason Hollinger)*

CLOCKWISE FROM RIGHT *Rosa eglanteria* is the 'trifecta rose'—beautiful, fragrant, edible. Sheep sorrel greens are best harvested before plants flower, when the leaves are at their largest. When you see a field tinged with patches of red, you may have found a stash of flowering sheep sorrel; come back a bit earlier next year!

CLOCKWISE FROM TOP Shotweed is best before it flowers. Look closely to see how sow thistle leaves grasp the stems. Sheep sorrel's lemony tartness breaks up the heavier flavor of smoked trout.

CLOCKWISE FROM TOP LEFT If you find a good patch, it only takes a few minutes to collect a large cache of stinging nettle. Wild carrot's lace-like flowers, better know as Queen Anne's lace, are typically white or cream colored, but are also sometimes tinged with pink. Look for the edible wild carrot's hairy stalk; poisonous hemlock look-alikes have smooth stalks.

CLOCKWISE FROM TOP LEFT Young wild fennel shoots sprouting in and around the previous year's stalks. Fennel cookies are delicious with a hint of anise flavor. Wild fennel fruits offer up a strong anise flavor, great for making aromatic infusions. OPPOSITE FROM TOP Wild mustard leaves are deeply serrated with backward-pointing segments. Wild mustard greens served Southern-style.

FROM TOP Wild pea flowers look very similar to garden sweet peas, only they grow in tangled mounds and lack a pleasant scent. Wild peas should be harvested when pods are green and plump.

Cut the sheet of puff pastry into four 4-inch squares. Lay one pastry square on baking sheet, then place a heaping tablespoonful of filling in center of the square. Fold the dough over the filling to form a triangle. Seal edges by pressing lightly with a fork. Repeat for remaining three squares. Brush the surfaces with the remaining egg mixture. Lightly sprinkle sesame seeds over each pastry.

Bake for 30 minutes, until golden brown. Serve hot or at room temperature.

Feast your eyes on these appetizing bourekas.

Dead Nettle

Red Dead Nettle, Purple Archangel, Henbit

Lamium purpureum

enjoy taking a close look at dead nettle now and then. The plant's flowers are arranged like small lavender pagodas with pink trumpets coyly peeking out from each level. If allowed to proliferate, they make a beautiful, albeit short-lived, ground cover.

Dead nettle is an annual herbaceous ground cover in the mint family (Lamiaceae). It is native to Europe and Asia but has spread throughout most of North America. According to Green Deane of eattheweeds.com fame, while many believe the word is derived from *lamium,* meaning "a thin layer, plate, or scale," *lamia* was the Greek term used for grotesque creatures. Literally it means "female man-eater." I agree with Deane that if you use your imagination, you can see how the flower resembles a creature preparing to pounce from its cave.

The common name dead nettle sounds a bit ominous, but it actually refers to an absence of stingers, so this plant can be eaten raw as well as cooked. Many people enjoy dead nettle raw, but because it has a flavor much like chard, a little bit goes a long way for me. However, I love eating it once it's cooked. Upon cooking, the tiny hairs disappear and the flavor is transformed into a very nice spinach-meets-stinging nettle.

Dead nettle is listed as an invasive species in several corn-belt states. Not put off by such categories, bees and butterflies consider it a favorite, both types of insects finding abundant nectar in its blossoms.

IN THE FIELD

What It Looks Like: Grows up to 12 inches tall. Stems square; leaves opposite, round to triangular, sparsely hairy, with scalloped edges. Lower leaves 1–1½ inches long, dull green; upper leaves smaller, more triangular, usually purplish red. Flowers red to purple, tubular, blooming year-round in mild climates, occurring in whorls of three to six among upper leaves. Roots fine and fibrous.

Where to Find: Occurs throughout the United States, except for Arizona, Florida, Hawaii, Minnesota, New Mexico, North Dakota, South Dakota, Texas, and Wyoming. Primarily found in turf grass, landscapes, fields, farmlands.

When to Harvest: Early spring through summer, before and during blooming.

What to Eat: Entire plant; top third is most commonly used.

How to Harvest: For best flavor, gather top third of plant (typically, red-to-purple portion).

Poisonous Look-Alikes to Avoid: None.

IN THE KITCHEN

Why You Should Eat It: High in iron. High levels of antioxidants in seed oil have been studied for use as a food additive and supplement.

What It Tastes Like: Like most of its relatives in the mint family, it features a strong smell and flavor. Though many enjoy it raw, it tastes like uncooked chard to me, a flavor somewhere between dirt and grass. However, when cooked, its flavor is more like stinging nettle, chard, or spinach: wonderful.

How to Store: Does not store well raw. Use immediately, or dry or blanch and freeze for long-term storage.

How to Cook: Use raw with other greens in salads. Use as a potherb or store for future use.

Dead Nettle and Winter Squash with White Truffle Oil and Hazelnuts

I just had to include one recipe with white truffle oil, since it's my favorite flavor on the planet, and this dish is perfect for it. The earthy flavor of the truffle oil is the perfect foil to the chard-like notes of dead nettle. Consumed slowly, mindfully even, this dish's flavors are complex and multilayered. NOTE: you'll need a 3-inch-high, 12-inch-diameter brazier pan, deep frying pan, or Dutch oven.

* SERVES 6 *

1 onion, halved and sliced thinly
1 tablespoon olive oil
1 clove garlic, minced
1 cup vegetable or chicken broth
2 pounds butternut squash, cut to 1-inch cubes
1 cup chardonnay, divided
2 cups loosely packed fresh dead nettle, rinsed, patted dry, and coarsely chopped
Salt and pepper to taste
¼ cup unsalted butter
2 tablespoons white truffle oil
½ cup hazelnuts, coarsely chopped

Sauté onions in olive oil on medium heat, just until soft. Add garlic, vegetable broth, squash, and ¾ cup wine. Cover and bring to a boil. Lower heat to medium low and simmer 10–15 minutes, until you can easily pierce the squash with a fork.

Add dead nettle and remaining ¼ cup white wine. Cover and simmer another 2–3 minutes, until dead nettle is tender. Uncover and season to taste. Cook uncovered for another 4–5 minutes, until most of the liquid has evaporated.

In a separate small pan or in a microwave, melt the butter. Remove from heat and whisk in truffle oil. Add butter mixture to dead nettle and squash mixture and gently toss. Serve topped with hazelnuts.

Dead Nettle Crisps

These make an excellent garnish, crouton, or snack. You can play with the spices in this recipe to create your own signature flavorings.

* MAKES 15 TO 20 *

Spray-on coconut oil
2 cups (15–20) dead nettle flower heads
Spray-on Bragg's liquid aminos
    (or tamari or soy sauce)
2 tablespoons curry powder
    (or your choice of spices)
3 tablespoons grated Romano cheese

Preheat oven to 425°F. Lightly coat a baking sheet with spray-on coconut oil. Place flowers, tips up and evenly spaced, on baking sheet. Spray each flower with a spritz of Bragg's liquid aminos. Spray each flower with a spritz of coconut oil.

Mix together curry powder and cheese, then use your fingers to sprinkle the mixture over each flower. Spray each flower with another quick spritz of coconut oil so the curry powder adheres. Bake for 2–3 minutes. Let cool and gently remove from pan.

Note: The baked flowers are fragile; handle gently if you want them to remain whole.

OPPOSITE Dead nettle looks a little like a miniature pagoda.

Mallow

Common Mallow, Button Weed, Cheese Mallow, Cheese Weed, Dwarf Mallow

Malva neglecta

The next time you see a clump of the humble common mallow, take a close look at the flower. If you look at it straight on, it looks much like its fancier relatives, hibiscus, hollyhock, and rose of Sharon. It can be difficult to identify mallow in your lawn for the first time, as usually the flowers are mown into submission. However, if you grow your lawn out a bit, you may eventually have mallow that blooms.

When I first learned about this plant, I was excited about the prospect of having an ingredient in my yard with which to make marshmallows, but it was not to be. Early marshmallows were made by whipping marsh mallow roots with sugar, then baking like a meringue. (Marsh mallow is the common name for *Althea officinalis*, also in the Malvaceae family.) Making marshmallows does not work well with *Malva neglecta*, and perhaps that's why she's so neglected. She does have her own culinary value, however.

Common mallow is an annual plant, although it sometimes sprouts a second year from a biennial root crown. Common mallow originated in Europe, Asia, and parts of Africa and was probably imported to North America by early European settlers as a medicinal herb. Common mallow is also known as buttonweed, cheeseplant, cheese weed, dwarf mallow, and roundleaf mallow. The word malva is derived from the Greek *malakos,* which means "soft," presumably a reference to its mucilaginous texture. *Neglecta* is Latin for "neglected," a name that comes up frequently for plants that grow in unintended areas. The word mallow comes from the Old English translation of malva, *malwe.*

Although often considered a weed, this plant has been consumed as a food for millennia. Mallows are some of the earliest cited plants in recorded literature. The ancient Roman poet Horace (65 BC–27 BC) referred to it as a staple food: *Me pascunt olivae, me cichorea, me malvae,* which translates to "as for me, olives, endives, and mallows provide sustenance." Another closely related mallow, *khubeza* in Arabic, is used as the main ingredient in a traditional Arab dish known by the same name. Arab people also use mallow in salads, soups, and other dishes. Known as *ebegümeci* in Turkey, mallow is used as a leafy green vegetable there.

It was also considered good medicine. According to Pliny the Elder (AD 23–79), whose 37-book *Natural History* was treated as scientific fact for centuries, mallow could cure all diseases of man. Celtic folk doctors used it as a remedy for hair loss, due to its downy hairs. Today, herbalists still regard mallow as an effective treatment for irritations of the mouth and other mucous membranes. It's also used for skin irritations, as well as for respiratory or digestive ailments.

IN THE FIELD

What It Looks Like: Spreading annual, sometimes biennial, typically 6 inches to 2 feet tall, with downy hairs. Young plants grow as basal rosettes. Leaves alternate and heart shaped to nearly round, about ½–1½ inches long, blunt- to sharp-toothed, shallowly lobed (five to seven lobes). Leaves appear crinkled as they unfurl. Flowers pale pink to nearly white, in loose clusters of one to three. Flowers resemble tiny hollyhock flowers. The five flower petals are obovate, about ⅜ inch long, notched at the tips. Each flower has numerous stamens conjoined into a tube at the base. Fruits are round capsules shaped like a wheel of cheese divided into wedges. Straight taproot with a coarsely branched secondary root system.

Where to Find: Occurs throughout the United States, except for Florida, Louisiana, and Mississippi. Common in turfgrass, landscapes, cultivated beds, nurseries, roadsides, railroads, waste places, cultivated fields. Grows best in well-drained soil.

When to Harvest: Flowers from June to September; seeds ripen from July through October.

What to Eat: Entire plant.

How to Harvest: All can be gathered by hand. Use a trowel or shovel to harvest roots.

Poisonous Look-Alikes to Avoid: None.

IN THE KITCHEN

Why You Should Eat It: Seeds contain 21 percent protein and 15.2 percent fat. Leaves are a good source of calcium, magnesium, potassium, iron, selenium, and vitamins A and C.

Who Should Avoid It: When grown on nitrogen-rich soils, especially conventionally farmed (versus organic) soils, the plant tends to concentrate high levels of nitrates in its leaves, which means it's best avoided by people with low levels of stomach acid. See Nitrates sidebar in chapter 1.

What It Tastes Like: A mild, pleasant flavor. Leaves mucilaginous. Immature seeds have a nutty flavor.

How to Store: Eat young seed heads and flowers soon after picking. Store leaves for several days in the refrigerator. Dry roots for future use.

How to Cook: Use leaves and young shoots raw in salads or cooked as any other leafy green. The mucilaginous leaves thicken soups and other foods in much the same way that okra does. Use roots to make an egg-white substitute that works well for baked meringue. Make a tea from the dried leaves. Use immature seeds raw or cooked.

Mallow Green Smoothie

Green smoothies are all the rage right now, and they should be. What an excellent way to incorporate leafy greens into your diet! I especially like adding mallow leaves to my green smoothies, as they give them a more puddinglike consistency than most other leaves will (see Other Weeds for a Green Smoothie for more weed ideas). Delicious and spectacularly healthy!

* MAKES 4 12-OUNCE SMOOTHIES *

2 bananas
1 cup frozen mangos
1 cup frozen blueberries
1 cup raw mallow leaves, packed
2 cups water, milk, or soymilk
Honey, maple syrup, or fruit jam to taste

Blend all ingredients until smooth using a blender or food processor. Serve cold.

Green smoothies don't necessarily come in shades of green; the addition of blueberries gives this one a lovely shade of lavender.

Mallow Seafood Gumbo

This is a very forgiving recipe, so feel free to substitute other ingredients. The mallow greens act as the perfect stand-in for the standard gumbo ingredient, okra, and give it a similar consistency. A mighty fine gumbo!

* SERVES 6 TO 8 *

¼ pound Italian sweet or spicy sausage, sliced

1 tablespoon olive oil

1 small onion, chopped

1 medium stalk celery, chopped

½ green bell pepper, cored, seeded, and chopped

3 14½-ounce cans chicken broth

1 28-ounce can crushed tomatoes

2 cups mallow leaves, tough stems removed

2 tablespoons all-purpose flour

½ cup water

1 tablespoon salt

¼ teaspoon pepper

1 tablespoon dried thyme

1 bay leaf

½ teaspoon dried oregano

½ teaspoon dried basil

1 teaspoon Creole (or Old Bay) seasoning

1 teaspoon Worcestershire sauce

4 scallions, finely chopped, about ½ cup

½ pound shrimp, peeled and deveined, cut into thirds

½ pound crabmeat

¼ cup chopped fresh parsley

Place sausage in a saucepan and fill with water to cover. Bring to a boil and cook for 3–4 minutes. Drain and set aside.

Heat oil in a large pot over medium-high heat. Add onion, celery, and green pepper and cook until softened (but not browned), about 5 minutes, stirring occasionally. Add chicken broth, tomatoes, mallow greens, and sausage, cover, and bring to a boil. Continue cooking, covered, over medium heat for 5 minutes.

In a small bowl, whisk together flour and ½ cup water. Stir the flour mixture, salt, spices, and Worcestershire sauce into the pot, cover, and cook over medium heat for another 10 minutes.

Add scallions, shrimp, and crabmeat, and cook for 5 minutes. Remove bay leaf, stir in parsley, and remove from heat. Cover and let sit for 5 minutes.

Serve alone or over rice. Note: Freezes well if you have leftovers (but you won't).

Other weeds for a green smoothie

Here are some wild leafy greens that are especially good in green smoothies:

Bedstraw	Linden leaves
Cat's ear	Nettle
Chickweed	Nipplewort
Clover	Pigweed
Creeping wood sorrel	Plantain
Dandelion	Purslane
Dead nettle	Rose shoots
Dock	Sheep sorrel
Lamb's-quarter	

Plantain

Common Plantain, Broadleaf Plantain
Plantago major

ere is yet another weed I suspect is familiar to most of us through some of our earliest memories. Unless you are looking at a lawn awash in chemical neatness, plantain is nearly *always* resident. I remember enjoying the sensation of grasping the tops of plantains, (mature dock was also good), and allowing the seeds to fall into my hand. Several plants later, I'd have an entire satisfying fistful to scatter to the ground—in all likelihood, directly onto my mother's vegetable garden; luckily, she never caught on to my contribution.

Plantain is another lawn weed that, unlike most grasses, survives the driest of summers. In late August, most lawns in Seattle are dry, colorless, and crispy. If you have a weedy lawn, however, you are at least blessed with a few green oases in your desert of what appears as dead grass. The more weeds, the greener the lawn, in fact. My own unkempt lawn is loaded with these little islands of green, compliments of plantain, cat's ear, dandelion, mallow, and clover. Someday I hope they crowd the grass out to the degree that I have a patch of green, drought-tolerant yard all summer long. It's less labor intensive and costly than growing grass and quite a bit less ridiculous than laying artificial turf or painting my tan lawn green with "grass paint."

Plantago major belongs to a genus of about 200 species of small, inconspicuous plants commonly called plantains. (They are no relation to plantain bananas.) Most are herbaceous perennial plants. Broadleaf plantain is native to Europe and Asia but has widely naturalized and can now be found on every continent. Various *Plantago* species, including *P. major,* have been used for millennia as both food and herbal remedies. Archaeologists have dated their use as far back as 6500 BC.

The ancients thought *P. major* looked like the sole of a foot—the word *plantago* is derived from the Latin word for "sole of the foot." Early Native Americans shared this perception and called plantain "white man's footsteps," an apt naming as now, no matter where you are, you only have to look down to see one.

Plantago didn't arrive on our shores by accident. Thinking ahead, European settlers intentionally brought with them this valuable food and medicinal plant. In fact, it is considered one of the first introduced plants to reach North America after European contact. Note that edibility, location, harvesting, cooking, and storage information for *P. major* is also applicable to narrow-leaf plantain, *P. lanceolata,* another species in the *Plantago* genus that is extremely common in North America and elsewhere on the planet.

Because it's widely naturalized around the world, it enjoys many common names, among them cart-track plant, dooryard plantain, greater plantago, healing blade, hen plant, lambs foot, roadweed, roundleaf plantain, snakeroot, waybread, and wayside plantain. One common name, soldier's herb, was bestowed for its historical use as a wound dressing on battlefields.

Besides healing wounds, *Plantago* has been used to treat snakebites, uterine bleeding, coughs, ulcers, ringworm, gallstones, jaundice, epilepsy, and hemorrhoids, among other things. Psyllium seed, a fiber supplement and bulk laxative commonly used today to treat constipation and diverticulosis, is derived from a plant in the *Plantago* genus; the seeds of *P. major* and *P. lanceolata* can be used similarly. Chaucer and Shakespeare both mention its common usage in foods and medicines, and many 14th- and 15th-century European cooking recipes included plantain.

In addition to its value as a food and medicine, common plantain leaves contain a fiber suitable for textiles, mucilage from the seed coatings is used in the production of fabric starch, and the whole plant is used to produce gold and brown dyes.

IN THE FIELD

What It Looks Like: Grows from fibrous root system into basal rosette of leaves. Leaves 2–6 inches long, oval with smooth edges, three to eight prominent parallel ribs. Leaves present April through October or longer in milder climates. Leafless flower stalks rise from center of rosette to height of 5–12 inches. Small, greenish-brown flowers produced in a dense, nearly solid spike-shaped cluster (inflorescence). Inflorescences typically rise well above leaves; comprised of numerous tiny flowers. Flowers pollinated by wind, insects, birds, other animals. Seeds become sticky when wet; transported by hooves, webbed feet, shoes. Seeds germinate in autumn of production or early the following year. Germination most successful where soils have been lightly compressed, such as by trampling. Main time frame for seedlings to emerge is January to April, but can emerge at any time. In mild climates, plants overwinter as small rosettes. Seed persistence in soil is estimated at 50–60 years. Not frost tender.

Where to Find: Both broadleaf and narrow-leaf plantain occur throughout the United States. Cosmopolitan; abundant along paths, roadsides, and other areas with lightly compacted soils. Common in lawns and agricultural crops. Tolerates a wide variety of soils. Does not tolerate full shade well.

When to Harvest: In spring when plants are tender. Later in summer, leaves are tougher but can be cooked to soften them. Collect young flower stalks while they are still tender. For roasted seeds, gather seed stalks through September.

What to Eat: Leaves, young inflorescences, seeds.

How to Harvest: By hand as you would any other leafy green.

Poisonous Look-Alikes to Avoid: None.

IN THE KITCHEN

Why You Should Eat It: High in vitamins A, C, and K. Also contains notable levels of calcium, phosphate, and potassium.

Who Should Avoid It: Some people may be allergic to the pollen of this plant. If a pollen allergy is suspected, avoid using the flower heads and seeds. Also, avoid harvesting from heavily fertilized fields as *P. major* is very effective at taking up nitrates. (See chapter 1 sidebar on nitrates.)

What It Tastes Like: Young, green inflorescences taste like a nutty corn on the cob. Roasted seeds have a nutty, buttery flavor. Young greens taste slightly like spinach; older leaves attain some bitterness. Steam, boil, or otherwise cook to reduce or remove bitterness and toughness.

How to Store: Dry leaves, seeds, and roots for herbal tea or freeze for later use. Store fresh greens in a loosely covered container in the refrigerator for several days. Store roasted seeds in airtight containers for up to a year.

How to Cook: Roast whole seed stalks and add to a variety of foods or grind into flour just prior to use. Sauté young flower stalks with other vegetables. Use leaves as you would any other leafy green such as spinach.

Plantain Pasta

This recipe works well with any of the greens discussed in this book. The pasta tastes much like store-bought spinach pasta, and it's another great way to incorporate leafy greens into your regular diet. It's also a fun way to get fussy eaters to try weed cuisine.

Note: You'll need a pasta machine; alternatively, you can use a rolling pin, cutting board, and sharp knife.

* MAKES ABOUT 1½ POUNDS FRESH PASTA *

½ pound fresh plantain greens
1½ cups unbleached all-purpose flour
2 large eggs

Steam plantain greens with a teaspoon of water in a sauté pan, just until wilted. Cool. Drain, then squeeze to remove all excess moisture. Finely mince.

Mound flour onto a work surface and make a well in the middle. Add eggs and finely chopped greens into the well. Using a fork, whisk eggs and greens together for a minute and gradually incorporate flour from inside edges of the well until eggs aren't runny.

Use your hands to continue working flour, eggs, and plantain leaves into a smooth, non-sticky dough. Knead dough for 5–10 minutes, until it is soft and smooth. (Knead by pushing the heel of your hand into the dough, then away from yourself. Fold dough in half and turn 90 degrees to push again.)

If you're using a pasta machine, set it on the largest opening. Cut the dough into six pieces and set aside under a towel. Flatten one piece with your hand until it feeds through the smooth thinning rollers. Fold the flattened strip into thirds and feed it through a second time at the same opening width, then lay the flattened pasta dough strip aside on a clean towel, covered with another towel. (Alternatively, you can use a rolling pin and a sharp knife to achieve the same effect.)

Repeat the process to flatten all the balls of dough through the widest setting. Lay them next to each other on the towel. Keep them separated so they don't stick. Narrow the roller width by one notch and roll each strip of dough again. Repeat, narrowing the rollers one setting at a time until the dough is the thickness you desire. Let the dough dry for about 15 minutes. Using the cutting side of the machine, cut to the desired width. Hang cut noodles over the back of a wooden kitchen chair. Use immediately, or dry thoroughly for storage.

To cook, bring a generous amount of salted water to a rolling boil. Drop noodles in and return to a boil. If using fresh pasta, cook for only about a minute. Check dried pasta for doneness after 3 minutes, then every couple minutes. Serve with any pasta sauce you desire.

Plantain Buds with Dried Apricot and Hazelnut Couscous

Young plantain buds have a novel look when served alone or as part of a dish. Because they take on the taste of their fellow ingredients, I like them with butter and garlic. Here I've added a few more ingredients for a delicious side dish. I generally serve it warm, but it also works well as a chilled salad.

* SERVES 4 *

2 cups plantain buds
2 cloves garlic
¼ cup butter
1⅓ cups uncooked couscous
1 teaspoon cumin
¼ cup seasoned rice vinegar
¼ cup olive oil
⅔ cup shelled pistachios
½ cup dried apricots, chopped
⅔ cup sweetened dried cranberries (Craisins)
3 scallions, chopped
Salt and fresh ground pepper to taste

Sauté plantain buds and garlic in butter on low heat until softened, about 5 minutes.

Prepare couscous according to package directions.

Whisk together cumin, vinegar, and olive oil. Toss vinegar mixture with pistachios, apricots, cranberries, and scallions; add sautéed plantain buds. Gently toss this mixture with cooked couscous until combined. Season to taste. Serve at room temperature or chilled.

Narrowleaf plantain (*P. lanceolata*) leaves are more narrow
than those of *P. major*, but both plants can be used similarly.

3 | VEGETABLE GARDENS AND FLOWER BEDS

Oh, the hours, the *days* I've spent on my hands and knees crawling through the dirt to rid my garden of weeds. Imagine my delight when I discovered that I love the flavor of shotweed, a plant I'd grown to detest for its prolific ability to reproduce in my otherwise clean, straight rows of vegetables. It wasn't long before we were eating most of the weeds we removed from the garden.

Of course, this invites the question, why not just grow gardens of weeds if you like them so well? It took awhile for my fairly conventional brain to embrace this concept, but eventually I gave in to common sense and did just that. I still have a vegetable garden, but now when I weed it, I carefully transplant the dandelions, pigweed, and lamb's-quarter to the weed garden. As it's becoming increasingly clear to me that nature produces much more abundantly if I just leave it alone, I predict that at some point I'll let go of the conventional gardening thing altogether.

Note that while the weeds in this chapter are common to gardens, they are also commonly found in many other urban places.

Amaranth

Pigweed, Red-Root Amaranth, Redroot Pigweed, Common Amaranth,
Careless Weed, Tumbleweed, Wild Spinach
Amaranthus retroflexus

used to think pigweed was the same thing as ragweed. Let me just say that the two are only alike in half a name. Pigweed does not share the undesirable allergen properties that ragweed does. In fact, it's a great substitute for people with gluten allergies and intolerances. Amaranth seed contains no gluten and is a popular substitute grain for individuals with celiac disease. In the mid-1980s, I went on a six-month gluten-free diet hoping to cure an undiagnosed digestive problem. Back then, if you wanted a gluten-free pastry, you had to find your own amaranth, quinoa, and millet, no easy feat. At the end of six months, I was so frustrated at not being able to find the necessary raw ingredients, I gave up. I suppose had I known our amaranth weeds were edible, I could have found or grown and harvested my own. It's relatively easy to go gluten free these days. There are now so many gluten-intolerant tummies around that amaranth-based breakfast cereal, flours, and baked goods can be found in all large grocery stores.

The amaranth genus is thought to have originated in the Americas, spreading to Europe, Asia, and Africa after colonization began. It includes nearly 70 species and, although in some places they are considered weeds, many cultures throughout the world value amaranths as leaf vegetables and cereals. It's a genus of few distinguishing characteristics, thus its taxonomy is complicated to decipher. Happily, there are no poisonous species.

The common name pigweed is thought to be based on farmers historically using amaranth as pig fodder. The word amaranth comes from the Greek word for "unfading," *amarantos,* and the Greek word for "flower," *anthos.* In ancient Greece, amaranth was believed to have special healing properties.

Known to the Aztecs as *huautli,* amaranth may have represented up to 80 percent of their caloric consumption before the Spanish conquest, archaeologists believe. During Huitzilopochtli, an Aztec festival honoring the blue hummingbird god, the Aztecs performed ritual dances, songs, and prayers and broke a month-long fast by eating a morsel of a statue of the god made from amaranth seeds and honey. After the Spanish conquest, cultivation of amaranth was outlawed as a means of abolishing pagan beliefs. Amaranth was also a staple food of the Incans.

Amaranths have been promoted for use in arid third-world countries because they are very drought tolerant, easily harvested by hand, an excellent source of protein, and easy to cook. Amaranths are rich in the very amino acids that other common grains, such as wheat and corn, are lacking, and thus are a good food to combine with other grains. Several species of amaranth are raised for abundant, tasty seeds (often referred to as grain or pseudo grain) in Asia and the Americas, though *Amaranthus retroflexus* is not grown commercially in the United States. Several amaranth species, including *A. retroflexus,* are cultivated and consumed as a leafy green in Indonesia, Malaysia, the Philippines, India, China, Vietnam, East Africa, Uganda, Nigeria, Trinidad, Jamaica, Greece, Sri Lanka, and Fiji.

In spite of their nutritional and culinary benefits, not all amaranth species are cultivated. Most of the species that occur in the United States are considered weeds and commonly referred to as pigweeds. These species have an extended period of germination, rapid growth, and high rates of seed production, and thus are considered a problem for farmers trying to grow a monoculture of something else. Pigweeds are seen as an increasing concern for farmers as the plants quickly evolve to resist today's pesticides (see Herbicide-Resistant Weeds in chapter 1). This is particularly true of the Powell's amaranth species, *Amaranthus powelli*, and Palmer's amaranth, *Amaranthus palmeri* (both of which have been cultivated as food in the past and currently are in some other countries). The pigweeds considered invasive or noxious weeds are *A. albus*, *A. blitoides*, *A. hybridus*, *A. palmeri*, *A. powelli*, *A. spinosus*, *A. tuberculatus*, *A. viridis*, and of course the pigweed described here, *A. retroflexus*. All are edible and highly nutritious.

In addition to their culinary uses, pigweeds can be useful to farmers as a beneficial weed or companion plant. They are good companion plants for onions, corn, tomatoes, and peppers. Their sturdy seedlings break up hard soil, and their deep roots bring minerals from lower levels of the soil to the surface, where they are available to plants with shallower root systems.

The amaranth genus also contains several well-known ornamental plants, such as *Amaranthus caudatus* (love-lies-bleeding), a native of India and a vigorous, hardy annual with dark purplish flowers crowded in handsome drooping spikes. The flowers of a red amaranth have long been used as a source of a deep red dye. Today, a synthetic dye originally named amaranth for its similarity in color to the natural amaranth pigments is known as Red No. 2. Better living through chemistry? Probably not.

IN THE FIELD

What It Looks Like: An erect, annual herb reaching a maximum height of nearly 9 feet. Leaves nearly 6 inches long on large plants, ones higher on the stem having a lance shape, those lower on plant diamond or oval in shape. Flowers borne at or near top of plant in large, dense clusters interspersed with spiny green bracts. Fruit a capsule, about 1/16 inch long, containing a single seed. Seeds tiny, about 1/32 inch in diameter, shiny dark brown to black in color. Plants frost tender.

Where to Find: Occurs throughout the United States. Common in fields, gardens, vacant lots. Tolerates most soils that are well draining in full to partial sunlight. Thrives in hot, sheltered locations.

When to Harvest: Throughout summer. Juvenile amaranth available as early as late May can be consumed whole. Later in July, mature plants acquire tough stems that should be boiled before eating. Flowers from July to September; seeds ripen from August to October.

What to Eat: Entire plant, but most foragers stick to leaves and seeds.

How to Harvest: Collect greens by hand as you would any other leafy green. To collect seeds, hold a seed head upside down in a paper or plastic bag and gently shake seeds loose. Seeds do not all ripen at once, so you can increase the yield from an individual plant by collecting seeds once a week. You can also harvest the entire seed head and let it dry indoors; shake seeds loose as described above.

Poisonous Look-Alikes to Avoid: None.

IN THE KITCHEN

Why You Should Eat It: Seeds a good source of iron, magnesium, phosphorus, copper, manganese, thiamine, niacin, riboflavin, folate, calcium, and zinc. According to US National Research Council, amaranth seeds have a protein content of about 16 percent, more than other widely consumed cereals such as conventional wheat, rice, or corn. Also, amaranth's protein digestibility score is an impressive 90 percent, much higher than foods such as soy, milk, and wheat that are often problematic. Amaranth seeds do not contain all of the essential amino acids but are rich in lysine, an amino acid that many other grains lack. Therefore, it's a good complementary cereal for combining to obtain the full suite of amino acids found in complete protein. Amaranth seeds contain 5–9 percent high-quality oil, again, much higher than other common cereals. Amaranth oil contains tocotrienols—a relatively rare and very beneficial form of vitamin E. Several studies have shown that, like oats, amaranth seed or oil may be of benefit for those with hypertension and cardiovascular disease; regular consumption reduces blood pressure and cholesterol levels while improving the immune system. Amaranth leaves high in vitamin A, vitamin C, and folate; also contain respectable levels of thiamine, niacin, riboflavin, calcium, iron, potassium, zinc, copper, and manganese.

Who Should Avoid It: Leaves may contain nitrates if grown in nitrate-rich soils such as on land where chemical fertilizers are used (see Nitrates sidebar in chapter 1). Leaves also contain oxalic acid and may be a concern to people with kidney problems (see Oxalic Acid sidebar in this chapter).

What It Tastes Like: Toasting the seeds improves their flavor but may reduce some vitamin content; however, toasting may make other nutrients more bioavailable. Cooked or raw, leaves taste like a strong spinach.

How to Store: Wrap fresh leaves loosely in a plastic bag with a damp paper towel. Store dried leaves in airtight containers for a year or longer.

How to Cook: As with garden spinach, eat young leaves raw or cooked. Eat seeds raw, cooked as a cereal, or ground into a flour substitute. They can also be sprouted for salads and sandwiches. In Mexico and parts of South America, amaranth grains are toasted much like popcorn and mixed with honey, molasses, or chocolate to make a treat called *alegría,* meaning "joy" in Spanish.

You can up your vitamin intake for spanikopita by making it the classic Cretan way: use wild greens instead of garden spinach.

Amaranth Spanikopita

Let's pretend amaranth is spinach. It can be used leaf for leaf in most recipes calling for spinach, including the classic Greek dish spanikopita. Your guests won't believe you when you tell them you collected a key ingredient from a vacant lot rather than a grocery store.

* MAKES 9 SERVINGS *

⅛ cup plus 2 tablespoons olive oil
1 shallot, chopped
6 scallions, chopped
2 cloves garlic, minced
1 pound amaranth, rinsed and chopped
¼ cup chopped fresh parsley
1 egg, lightly beaten
¼ cup ricotta cheese
½ cup crumbled feta cheese
8 sheets phyllo dough

Preheat oven to 350°F. Oil a 9-by-9-inch square baking pan.

Heat 2 tablespoons olive oil in a large skillet over medium heat. Sauté shallot, scallions, and garlic until soft. Add amaranth and parsley. Continue to sauté until amaranth is limp, about 2 minutes. Remove from heat and set aside to cool.

In a medium bowl, mix together egg, ricotta, and feta, then stir it into the spinach mixture.

Lay a sheet of phyllo dough in the prepared baking pan and brush lightly with olive oil. Lay another sheet of phyllo dough on top and brush with olive oil. Repeat this process with two more sheets of phyllo. The sheets will extend beyond the edges of the pan.

Spread the amaranth and cheese mixture into the pan and fold overhanging dough over filling. Brush with oil, then layer remaining four sheets of phyllo dough, brushing each with oil. Tuck overhanging dough into pan to seal filling.

Bake in preheated oven for 30–40 minutes, until golden brown. Cut into nine squares. Serve immediately.

Note: To prevent a soggy bottom, drain and cool the filling completely and assemble with phyllo dough just before baking. Alternatively, sprinkle a layer of dried bread crumbs atop the bottom crust before filling.

Amaranth and Caramelized Onions on Sourdough

This recipe makes a simple but delectable sandwich that will appeal to vegans, vegetarians, and omnivores alike.

* SERVES 4 *

4 cups thinly sliced onion
3 teaspoons olive oil, divided
2 teaspoons sugar
1 loaf sourdough French bread
2 cups loosely packed amaranth, chopped
Kosher salt and freshly ground pepper to taste

Combine onion, 2 teaspoons oil, and sugar in a large skillet. Cover and cook over low heat for 15 minutes. Uncover and turn the heat to medium-high. Cook, stirring frequently, 5–10 minutes longer, until browned.

Meanwhile, slice loaf horizontally, not cutting all the way through, starting on one long side. Open bread and press down to flatten.

Add amaranth to onions and cook just until wilted. Spread amaranth mixture on bottom half of bread and sprinkle with salt and pepper. Drizzle with remaining olive oil. Close loaf and press down. Slice into four sandwiches and serve.

*Yet well I ken the banks
where Amaranths blow,
Have traced
the fount whence streams
of nectar flow.
Bloom, O ye Amaranths!
bloom for whom ye may,
For me ye bloom not! Glide,
rich streams, away!*

—Samuel Taylor Coleridge,
Work Without Hope (1825)

Once the amaranth flower head is nearly dry, harvest seeds by shaking them into a paper bag. Seeds that drop on the ground will guarantee you a healthy crop for the next growing season.

Creeping Wood Sorrel

Oxalis, Procumbent Yellow-Sorrel, Sleeping Beauty
Oxalis corniculata

n the Pacific Northwest, *Oxalis oregano* forms emerald-green carpets in older-growth forests, particularly in Olympic National Park's rain forests. It is one of the first western Washington plants I learned about when I returned to Olympia as an adult, and I often nibbled at its lemony leaves while backpacking.

For years, I've been removing from my garden a smaller version of this native plant, *Oxalis corniculata,* or creeping wood sorrel. After learning about our native oxalis, it occurred to me that this weed might be edible. My garden hosts both green and purple varieties, and I was hoping to add the latter to our salads for its beautiful color. What a pleasant surprise to learn that it's edible and tastes just like the native, but a little less tart. Because it's impossible to rid my garden of it, I now happily add it to our salads regularly.

Oxalis corniculata is an herbaceous perennial plant. It is in the genus *Oxalis,* by far the largest genus in the wood-sorrel family Oxalidaceae, with 800 out of the total 900 species. The *Oxalis* genus occurs throughout most of the world, except for the polar areas. It is fully established around the globe, especially in cool and temperate regions. Species diversity is especially varied in Mexico, South America, and Africa. *Oxalis corniculata* (and its variant, *atropurpurea*) is thought to have originated in Europe, though from which area it spread is unknown. It probably migrated to the United States with explorers, as the small seeds easily stow away in bags of grain.

The common name sorrel is used because oxalis has a lemony taste similar to that of sheep sorrel, which is in the separate Polygonaceae family. Several *Oxalis* species are commonly referred to as shamrocks and are sold as potted plants, especially around St. Patrick's Day. The word sorrel is from the High German word *sur* meaning "sour," while the word oxalis comes from oxys, the Greek word for "pungent," "sharp," or "acidic."

Nearly the entire *Oxalis* genus is edible and, according to the website Plants for a Future (www.pfaf.org), none are poisonous. In fact, various *Oxalis* species have been consumed by humans around the world for millennia. The Potawatomi Indian tribe used it to make a dessert. For centuries, *O. tuberose (oca)* has been cultivated for its edible tuber in Colombia and elsewhere in the Andes mountains of South America. Today in India, *O. corniculata* is known as *chichoda bhaji* ("earth-almond greens") and is eaten seasonally beginning in December.

Medicinally, the Kiowa Indian tribe used it to alleviate thirst on long trips, the Algonquin as an aphrodisiac, the Cherokee to alleviate mouth sores and sore throat, and the Iroquois to treat cramps, fever, and nausea. Herbalists use several *Oxalis* species in the treatment of flu, fever, urinary tract infections, enteritis, diarrhea, traumatic injuries, sprains, and poisonous snake bites. The juice of the plant, mixed with butter, is applied to muscular swellings, boils, and pimples. An infusion has been used to rid children of hookworms. Juice from the leaves is antibacterial and applied to insect bites, burns, and skin eruptions.

Some *Oxalis* species are hyperaccumulators of copper, so much so that the Chinese Ming dynasty used *O. corniculata* to locate copper deposits. For this reason, today it is thought to have some potential as a contaminated-soil phytoremediation plant.

What It Looks Like: Somewhat delicate-appearing, low-growing, with narrow, creeping stems that readily root at nodes. Grows to 4 inches tall; can be found in mounds measuring up to a foot in diameter. Trifoliate leaves subdivided into three rounded leaflets resembling a clover in shape. Some varieties have green leaves; variant *atropurpurea*'s leaves are purple. Leaves of purple variant usually flat; leaves of other forms slightly flexed from the center. Both variants have yellow flowers in bloom June to September. Fruit a narrow, cylindrical capsule ½–1 inch long known for its explosive discharge of its ⅟₃₂-inch-long tiny seeds. Flowers hermaphrodite, self-fertile, and pollinated by insects. Plant not frost tender.

Where to Find: Throughout North America; occurs throughout the United States, except for Colorado, Iowa, Kansas, Minnesota, and Nebraska. Flourishes in a variety of soils and conditions, though does poorly in shade or dry soils.

When to Harvest: Spring, summer, early fall.

What to Eat: Leaves, stems, flowers.

How to Harvest: Pinch off entire plants from stems at the bases, later removing any tough stems.

Poisonous Look-Alikes to Avoid: None.

Why You Should Eat It: High in vitamins C and A.

Who Should Avoid It: Contains oxalic acid, which may be a concern to people prone to kidney stones (see Oxalic Acid sidebar).

What It Tastes Like: All plants in this genus contain oxalic acid, giving the leaves and flowers a pleasantly sour taste. Perhaps simply due to its diminutive size, *O. corniculata*'s bite seems less sour than that of some of its larger relatives.

How to Store: Wrap loosely and store in refrigerator for several days.

How to Cook: Eat raw or cooked. Add to salads, cook as a potherb, or use to add citrus flavoring to other foods. Dry leaves for a lemony-tasting tea. Makes an excellent stuffing or sauce for fish and meat. Flowers generally used raw as a colorful addition to a salad.

Creeping Wood Sorrel German Potato Salad

Here is a fun, fruity version of a classic salad. Creeping wood sorrel's tart, lemony flavor is a welcome addition to the familiar flavors of German potato salad. It's also excellent in the traditional mayonnaise-based potato salad.

* SERVES 4 *

6 medium-size red potatoes (peels on), quartered
1 teaspoon salt
2 pieces bacon, chopped to 1-inch pieces
1 small onion, diced
¼ cup apple cider vinegar
2 tablespoons water
3 tablespoons raw sugar
salt and pepper to taste
1 cup loosely packed creeping wood sorrel greens

Place potatoes in a pot and fill with enough water to cover. Add salt. Bring to a boil and cook for about 15–20 minutes or until easily pierced with a fork. Drain and set aside to cool to room temperature.

In a large, deep skillet, fry bacon on medium-high heat until browned and crisp, turning as needed. Remove bacon and set aside. Add onion to bacon grease, and cook over medium heat until browned.

Add vinegar, water, sugar, salt, and pepper to the pan. Bring to a boil, then add potatoes. Crumble in half the bacon and transfer to a large bowl. Mix in creeping wood sorrel greens just prior to serving to preserve color and flavor. Top with remaining bacon and serve at room temperature.

Creeping Wood Sorrel Cooler

If life gives you lemons, make lemonade. But if it gives you a patch of creeping wood sorrel, grab a couple of handfuls and cool off with this tart, fruity concoction. Rather than the same old lemonade stand, maybe your youngsters would enjoy selling these coolers. Heck, customers might buy just to satisfy their curiosity.

* SERVES 6 TO 8 *

2 quarts water
1 cup creeping wood sorrel leaves
    (stems, flowers, and seedpods also fine)
2–4 tablespoons agave nectar or honey,
    to taste
Dash of salt

Mix all ingredients in a blender. If desired, remove pulp using cheesecloth or a fine sieve. For best flavor, make ahead and allow it to rest in the refrigerator overnight. Serve very cold.

Risks associated with plants containing oxalic acid

Many foraging resources contain conflicting information about oxalic acid. While my explanation is a bit technical, it aims to clear up any concerns you might have about eating plants that contain it.

Oxalic acid is a strong organic acid found in many plants. It's especially common in plants related to spinach and rhubarb. When oxalic acid bonds with calcium and other minerals, the resulting compounds are known as oxalate salts. Some oxalate salts are fairly water soluble, but calcium oxalate readily precipitates out of solution. The resulting solids can aggravate pre-existing conditions such as rheumatism, arthritis, gout, kidney stones, or hyperacidity. If you suffer from one of these conditions, you should avoid eating creeping wood sorrel and other plants containing oxalic acid.

Having said that, let's put things in perspective. Oxalic acid is very common in the American diet. Other foods with concentrations similar to those found in creeping wood sorrel include beet greens, leeks, okra, spinach, sweet potatoes, swiss chard, lentils, potatoes, beer, and chocolate.

Many sources also claim that oxalic acid robs the body of calcium. This simply isn't true.

Some plants, including several common house plants, contain the already formed calcium oxalate *crystals* in their leaves and stems. If ingested, these crystals can cause intense pain and swelling, difficulty swallowing, and temporary hoarseness. Because the intense mouth pain usually prevents one from eating a significant quantity of the plant, poisoning is rare.

The upshot?

- If you suffer from kidney stones or other kidney problems, avoid foods containing oxalic acid.
- If you do not suffer from kidney problems, you can include these foods as long as they're part of a balanced diet.
- Whether your kidneys function well or not, don't bother with plants containing calcium oxalate crystals.

Daylily

Tawny Daylily, Common Daylily
Hemerocallis fulva

Both my paternal and maternal grandmothers lived in rural Wisconsin, not far from where I lived during my teen years, and both of them had large patches of tawny daylilies marking the ends of their driveways. I rather doubt my grandmothers planted them, however; these lilies grew like weeds in the nearby ditches. They may have been planted way back when the places were homesteaded. More likely, they popped up at the edge of the yard and my grandmothers (who both did most of the lawn mowing) found themselves mowing around the clumps repeatedly until they'd grown to gigantic daylily patches. My grandmothers were both sharp as tacks, and I'm sure they recognized that more flowers meant less mowing. I wish they were both alive so that I could tell them about the virtues of daylilies as a food. Had they known how tasty they are, I'm sure both of them would have eaten them regularly.

The tawny daylily is a clump-forming, herbaceous perennial. Its genus name, *Hemerocallis,* comes from the Greek words for "day" and "beautiful," probably because the lovely blossoms last a mere 24 hours or so. There are now more than 60,000 registered *Hemerocallis* cultivars, many of which are edible. *Hemerocallis* was formerly part of the Liliaceae family (which includes the *Lilium* genus, true lilies) but was changed to the Xanthorrhoeaceae family, subfamily Hemerocallidoideae. *Hemerocallis fulva* is native to China, Korea, and Japan.

In China, the daylily has many names. When it assumes a cheerful position, the flower is called Wong Yu, meaning "forgetting worries." It's called I Nan, meaning "suited for a boy," when used by expectant women to increase the odds of having a baby boy. The Chinese also enjoy the daylily as a symbol of devotion to one's mother.

Tawny daylily is not only a versatile wild edible but a beautiful and easily grown perennial garden flower. It is sometimes called the Outhouse Lily because people often planted them around their outhouses.

IN THE FIELD

What It Looks Like: Grows in clumps up to 3 feet in diameter, each plant having leaves, a crown, flowers, and roots. Very young leaves look like flattened thumbs pointing in opposite directions. Daylily is not a true lily; blossoms not spotted, stems leafless. Flat, narrow, lanceolate leaves 1–3 feet long grouped into opposite fans with arching leaves. Leaves slightly folded with a central ridge running lengthwise down back of leaf. Stems smooth, round, leafless, branched at top, growing 2–3 feet tall. A few small, leaflike bracts may develop in upper portion of stem. Several flowers borne in a cluster at top of stem. Flowers typically have three petals, each with a midrib that is sometimes a contrasting color, and six stamens, each with a two-lobed anther. Flowers orange, funnel-shaped, unspotted, each opening for only one day. After successful pollination, flowers form capsules. Although the term "daylily bulb" is often used to describe dormant daylily roots, they are not true bulbs but, rather, tubers. Hardy to zone 4 and not frost tender.

Where to Find: According to USDA, naturalized in every state except Arizona, California, Hawaii, Nevada, New Mexico, North Dakota, and Oklahoma; in those states you may encounter it in flower gardens. Grows best in rich, damp, gravelly soil and can tolerate full sun to partial shade.

When to Harvest: Shoots and leaves best in early spring through mid-May, flower buds and flowers from May through mid-July. Tubers can be dug up any time of year that soil is workable.

What to Eat: Young leaves, shoots, flower buds, flowers, tubers.

How to Harvest: Using scissors, take center leaves or shoots when young; plant will continue to send up new growth. When digging up tubers, leave fibrous roots behind so plant continues to produce. If you remove an entire plant, don't worry: daylilies like to be thinned. Also be sure that you're not digging up any neighboring lilies or irises, which may be poisonous.

Poisonous Look-Alikes to Avoid: Other lilies, daffodils, irises. When in bloom, plant easily recognized by its six "petals" (technically, tepals). If plant not yet in bloom, perhaps easiest way to tell from poisonous look-alikes is to check roots. Common daylilies propagate from an underground network of tubers that resemble very small potatoes, whereas poisonous look-alikes arise from individual bulbs or lateral rhizomes.

Daylily tubers resemble very small potatoes.

Note that some people are allergic to tawny daylilies and experience diarrhea and vomiting after eating them (particularly the tubers), so it's best to sample a small amount first. In addition, some reports warn that consuming large quantities of the young shoots can be hallucinogenic.

Very rarely, daylily tubers produce a toxin that, if eaten in quantity, can cause vomiting and diarrhea. This is such a rare occurrence that almost none of the literature even mentions it. The development of this transient characteristic may be due to specific weather patterns and seasonal rainfall. I had it happen to me once with tubers from a patch that I'd safely harvested from for years. It could be marketed as the ultimate cleanse, so if it happens to you, be sure to replenish your electrolytes and wait a couple years to try again, or find your tubers elsewhere. (For more on this see Safety in chapter 1.)

IN THE KITCHEN

Why You Should Eat It: Fairly high in calcium and vitamins A and C; flowers and buds high in iron.

What It Tastes Like: Young shoots and leaves mild with firm texture; hold up very well after cooking. Firm but tender, they taste slightly like corn silk. Flowers taste more like sweet lettuce and are somewhat mucilaginous. Tubers taste like mild, sweet turnips, slightly buttery.

How to Store: Place leaves and shoots in refrigerator in a loosely closed plastic bag with a damp paper towel. Dry buds and blossoms for long-term storage. Use fresh flowers or buds the same day they're picked.

How to Cook: The Chinese cook with daylily flowers regularly in dishes like moo shu pork and hot and sour soup; in Asian food stores, dried flowers are sold as "golden needles." Pull flower petals apart and add to salads or as an appealing garnish for any dish. Sauté the plump flower buds as well as opened flowers or add to stir-fries. Stuff fresh flowers, as you would squash blossoms. Like squash flowers, daylilies' flavor is very mild, but they are a bit more substantial than squash flowers and can feel slightly gelatinous in your mouth. Older tubers develop a transparent, papery covering; once tubers are cooked, easily squeeze them out of this skin.

Daylilies with Ginger
and Red Bell Peppers on Rice

Daylilies are a common ingredient in Asian cooking. This recipe is an amalgamation of a number of Chinese dishes I've had the pleasure of eating in Seattle's International District. It is as flavorful as it is easy to prepare.

* SERVES 4 *

½ teaspoon salt
1½ cups rice
3 cups water
1 tablespoon rice wine vinegar
1 tablespoon soy sauce
1 tablespoon water
1 tablespoon sugar
1 tablespoon vegetable oil
1 teaspoon grated fresh ginger
1 red bell pepper, cut into long, thin slices
3 cups fresh daylily buds

Cook rice according to the directions on the package.

Meanwhile, combine vinegar, soy sauce, water, and sugar until dissolved. Five minutes before the rice is done, heat oil in a wok or heavy skillet over high heat until very hot. Add ginger and stir briefly. Add red bell peppers and stir a few times quickly. Stir in vinegar mixture. Toss in daylily buds to mix well. Cook just until daylily buds are heated through. Serve with hot rice.

Daylilies and Raspberry Sorbet

In my experience, the simple beauty of daylily flowers makes any dessert all the more tempting. This recipe is so lovely to look at you'll probably have to remind your guests to eat it before the sorbet melts.

* SERVES 6 *

6 tawny daylily flowers
3 cups raspberry sorbet
¾ cup fresh raspberries
6 sprigs fresh mint or peppermint

Pick several large daylily flowers in the morning. Wash them and remove the stamens. Refrigerate in a covered bowl.

When it's time for dessert, place each daylily flower in a goblet. Fill each with ½ cup raspberry sorbet. Top each with ⅛ cup fresh raspberries and a sprig of mint. Serve immediately.

After seeing many of the 60,000 or so registered daylily cultivars, I still find the tawny daylily to be one of the most beautiful.

Lamb's-Quarter

White Goosefoot, Fat Hen
Chenopodium album

f you raise vegetables, I am almost certain you are familiar with this most tenacious weed. It loves moist, disturbed soil, and if you let even one of them go to seed, you will have a robust crop of it come springtime.

In much of North America, summer is a rather slow time for wild food foragers. The bountiful spring harvest is over, and comparatively few plants can be found during the hotter months. However, just as the spring plants are becoming too tough to eat, lamb's-quarters are maturing in abundance.

Chenopodium album is a fast-growing herbaceous annual. The word *chenopodium* is Greek for "goose foot," and indeed the shape of the leaves in this family do resemble goose feet. Other common names include white goosefoot and fat hen. It is sometimes also called pigweed, though that name is also commonly used for *Amaranthus albus*. The word lamb's-quarter may be a corruption of Lammas quarter, an August harvest festival that marked a quarter of the year, a pagan festival during which bread containing lamb's-quarter seeds was served.

Chenopodium has been found by archaeologists in ancient Roman sites in Europe. *C. album*'s native range is unclear due to its extensive cultivation over the centuries, but it's thought to include most of Europe and parts of Asia. Lamb's-quarter was brought to North America as a food plant; pioneers added the seeds to breads, pancakes, muffins, and cookies. Now it is widely naturalized in Africa, Australia, and North America, occurring in all 50 states and throughout most of Canada. Today, lamb's-quarter is extensively cultivated and consumed as a grain and vegetable in northern India, Asia, and Africa. In fact, in English texts it's often referred to by its Hindi name *bathua* or *bathuwa*.

Lamb's-quarter is closely related to a plant many of us are familiar with in the grocery store, amaranth. *Amaranthus* species are a popular wheat substitute for people who are allergic to gluten or whose systems don't tolerate it well. Both *Chenopodium* and amaranth are in the Amaranthaceae family. Amaranth has been cultivated as a grain for at least 8000 years. (A staple food of the Aztecs, its growth was banned by the conquistadors.) *C. album* is also closely related to quinoa, another amaranth superfood now commonly seen in grocery stores and better restaurants. (See this chapter for more about amaranth.)

Lamb's-quarter has enjoyed a few other uses beyond its edibility. It can be used as poultry food. The hardened stems were used as walking sticks in ancient China. It is used as a medicinal plant in traditional African medicine. Lastly, some herbalists recommend chewing it raw to soothe toothaches.

In North America, lamb's-quarter is considered merely a weed and is listed as a top plant threat to farmers. Some weed scientists estimate that, in the absence of chemical controls, lamb's-quarter could reduce corn crop production by 13 percent, soybeans by 25 percent, and sugar beets by 48 percent. Most farmers try to control lamb's-quarter through the use of preemergent chemical herbicides, but to varying degrees of success. Lamb's-quarter is now resistant to many herbicides and, in a growing number of places, has become resistant to glyphosate (Roundup). See Chemical Warfare in chapter 1.

Many organic farmers, on the other hand, consider lamb's-quarter a beneficial companion plant. Because it's vulnerable to leaf miners, it can be used as a pest-trap crop in spinach fields. Similarly, as a host plant for the beet leafhopper, it can be planted near beet fields as a pest-trap crop. (Beets and spinach are also in the chenopodium family.)

In his best-seller *In Defense of Food,* Michael Pollan calls out lamb's-quarter as one of the "most nutritious plants in the world." I wonder how many tons of this nutritious food we waste each year in order to protect the monocultured vegetables we're more comfortable with.

IN THE FIELD

What It Looks Like: Typically reaches heights of 2–3 feet, but in right conditions grows to 6–7 feet tall. Leaves alternate, light green, rounded, triangular (like a goose's foot), 1¼–10 inches long, on a long leaf stem (petiole). Center leaves have a distinctive white powdery look. Branching stems hairless, grooved, light green with occasional red coloration. Flowers very small, green, lacking petals, borne in tight clusters at tips of branches and upper leaf nodes. Seeds minuscule, black, round, shiny, with each plant capable of producing many thousands of seeds; average-size lamb's-quarter produces about 75,000 seeds. Seeds remain viable to 20 years and can grow in many soil types. Plants grow from a short, well-branched taproot.

Where to Find: All 50 states and throughout most of Canada. Typically in croplands, gardens, orchards, vineyards, landscaped areas, roadsides, other disturbed areas.

What to Eat: Leaves, flowers, young stems, seeds.

When to Harvest: Collect in late spring and throughout summer. In late spring, tender young plants can be used whole with washed roots left intact. As plants get older, taller, and tougher, gather tender tops for raw dishes such as salad. If you continue to do this, you will be rewarded with new tender leaves every couple weeks. Use any leaves that have become tough in cooked dishes. Harvest leaves until a heavy frost. In the fall, stems often become red-streaked and seed clusters turn reddish-brown; this means seeds are mature and ready to harvest.

How to Harvest: Collect leaves and flowers as you would any other leafy green. To collect seeds, carefully place a plastic bag over seed heads, invert, and shake.

Poisonous Look-Alikes to Avoid: Some sources list nettleleaf goosefoot, *Chenopodium murale,* as a poisonous look-alike. However, *C. murale* is in fact edible if properly prepared and not eaten in quantity. If eaten in quantity, *C. murale* can be mildly toxic due to its saponin and oxalic acid content (see Oxalic Acid and Saponin Sidebars in this chapter). However, its foul odor easily distinguishes it from *C. album.*

IN THE KITCHEN

Why You Should Eat It: Seeds high in protein, vitamin A, calcium, phosphorus, potassium. Leaves high in vitamins A and C, riboflavin, niacin, calcium, manganese, potassium, and iron. Also a good source of protein and fiber.

Who Should Avoid It: Contains oxalic acid, nitrates, and saponins, all of which can be toxic *if* eaten in large amounts. Very efficient at taking up metals, thus caution should be exercised when collecting it in urban or industrial areas. Finally, lamb's-quarter can absorb high levels of nitrates from heavily fertilized soils, so be aware of where you're collecting. See Oxalic Acid and Saponin sidebars in this chapter, as well as the Nitrates sidebar in chapter 1 for more about risks.

What It Tastes Like: A close relative to spinach, this plant tastes very much like its cousin—only better.

How to Store: Store dried seeds in an airtight container for up to a year. Store leaves in plastic bags or a loosely covered bowl in the refrigerator for up to a week. Dry leaves and store in jars. Steam or boil leaves, buds, and shoots and freeze for up to a year.

How to Cook: Eat leaves and young shoots as a leafy green. Leaves alone are best used like spinach, raw or cooked. Seeds are excellent whole or ground in breads, muffins, cakes, and pancakes; they can also be sprouted through winter.

Like its commercially available cousin quinoa, seed coatings of lamb's-quarter are high in saponins and therefore bitter and potentially toxic if consumed in large amounts. One means of removing the offensive hulls is to roast seeds lightly, then place them between two dish towels and apply pressure with a rolling pin. Once hulls are loose, winnow seeds repeatedly to blow bitter dust away (I have successfully used a hair dryer on a low setting). Then rinse seeds in a couple changes of water and dry them (see Saponins sidebar).

Lamb's-Quarter Pizza

I like putting something green on a pizza. It turns what I normally consider junk food into something closer to health food. And because lamb's-quarter is a close relative of spinach, I find nobody even notices if I substitute it in a dish calling for spinach. If you're having any trouble getting your children to sample weed cuisine, put a piece of this pizza in front of them. I just bet they'll change their minds. This recipe uses a kosher, unleavened flat bread (no yeast or sourdough) for the crust.

* MAKES 4 SMALL PIZZAS *

DOUGH

4 cups whole wheat flour
1½ teaspoons salt
3 tablespoons butter
2 egg yolks
2 tablespoons vegetable oil
1 cup milk

TOPPING

1½ pounds fresh lamb's-quarter leaves
2 tablespoons extra virgin olive oil, divided
1 cup shredded mozzarella cheese, divided
½ cup crumbled goat feta
¼ teaspoon each salt and pepper
¼ cup well-drained, coarsely chopped sun-dried tomatoes preserved in oil
¼ cup chopped green onions
¼ cup coarsely chopped kalamata olives
1 teaspoon minced fresh basil
1 teaspoon balsamic vinegar
1 garlic clove, minced

Preheat oven to 400°F. To make the dough, in a bowl combine flour and salt. Using a stand electric mixer with a dough hook, beat butter, egg yolks, and vegetable oil until combined (not smooth). Slowly add flour mixture alternately with milk while mixer is on medium-low speed. (Ingredients can also be combined by hand.) Dough should be crumbly but moist. Lightly knead dough by hand to form smooth ball.

Lightly flour a breadboard and pinch off a quarter of the dough. Pat the dough into a flat disk, then use a rolling pin to thin the disk to approximately ⅛ inch, keeping the board floured and flipping disk as necessary to avoid sticking. Repeat to make four crusts. Carefully transfer them to ungreased baking sheets. Lightly pierce surface of bread with a fork to help prevent bubbling.

In a large skillet, sauté lamb's-quarter on medium heat in 1 tablespoon olive oil for 1–2 minutes, until wilted. Let cool.

In a large bowl, combine ¼ cup each of mozzarella and goat cheese. Add lamb's-quarter, salt, and pepper and toss. Spread over crusts to within ½ inch of edge.

In a large bowl, combine tomato, green onions, olives, basil, 1 tablespoon olive oil, vinegar, and garlic. Sprinkle over pizzas. Top with remaining goat and mozzarella cheeses. Bake on center racks for 12–14 minutes or until cheese softens and is lightly browned. Cut into wedges and serve hot.

Lamb's-Quarter Farfalle Greek-Style

This is a light, healthy meal. Adding greens to pasta has to be one of the simplest ways to incorporate leafy greens into a meal. I usually throw the greens in with my pasta just before I drain it. By adding greens, I'm adding extra nutritional value and perking up the color and flavor of the dish.

* SERVES 4 *

1 pound farfalle pasta (butterflies)
3 tablespoons olive oil
3 large garlic cloves, minced
1 15-ounce can chickpeas, drained
½ cup chicken or vegetable broth
½ cup chardonnay
½ teaspoon dried oregano
½ teaspoon salt
½ teaspoon freshly ground pepper
1 pound fresh lamb's-quarter leaves,
**   trimmed and coarsely chopped**
¼ cup crumbled feta cheese

Cook the pasta in boiling water until al dente, then drain and rinse with cool water to stop further cooking. Set aside.

Heat oil in a large nonstick skillet over high heat. Add garlic and cook about 2 minutes, stirring frequently, until garlic begins to brown. Add chickpeas and mix to coat. Add broth, wine, oregano, salt, and pepper and bring to a boil. Reduce heat, cover, and let simmer 2 minutes.

Mix in pasta and lamb's-quarter and cook until pasta has absorbed most of the liquid and lamb's-quarters are fully wilted. Sprinkle with feta cheese and serve.

What are saponins?

Saponins, phytochemicals with foaming characteristics, are found in many familiar vegetables, beans, and herbs. The foaming ability of saponins is caused by the combination of a hydrophobic (fat-soluble) sapogenin and a hydrophilic (water-soluble) sugar. The best-known sources of saponins are peas, spinach, asparagus, oats, soybeans, and plants with names hinting at their foaming properties, such as soapwort, soaproot, soapbark, and soapberry.

Saponins have a bitter taste, and some are toxic in relatively small amounts. All are toxic in large amounts, though many are currently being studied for their potential medicinal uses. Scientists hope to confirm that saponins benefit high cholesterol, cancer, bone density, and stimulation of the immune system. To remove saponin's potentially bitter flavor, many sources recommend rinsing plants several times before cooking.

Saponins from commercially grown yucca and quillaja are used in some beverages, such as beer, to produce a stable foam. The detergent properties of saponins have also led to their use in shampoos, facial cleansers, and cosmetic creams.

OPPOSITE Lamb's-quarter flower buds

Purslane

Common Purslane, Verdolaga, Pigweed, Little Hogweed, Pusley, Green Purslane

Portulaca oleracea

Unless you are specifically looking for purslane, it is easy to pass it by repeatedly without ever noticing it. Unless you're at a trendy eatery, that is. As with pea shoots, purslane is one of the latest fashionable ingredients now used by some of our most talented culinary wizards, and it's very noticeable on the dinner plate. If a purslane plant could think (and, for all we know, it can), its recent popularity must have come as quite a surprise considering it's so easily overlooked in the urban landscape.

Purslane, a sprawling plant of lawns and meadows, is an herbaceous annual plant in the Portulacaceae family. It thrives in poor soils and is best known for its tart, succulent leaves and stems ("succulent" meaning water-containing or fleshy.) Purslane reminds me of miniature jade plants and, as such, would be a perfect choice for the bonsai gardener. Those puffy leaves are not only tasty, they happen to be a very rich source of omega-3 fatty acids.

The genus name, *Portulaca,* is from the Latin word *portula,* which means "gate," probably from the gatelike covering of the seed capsule. The species name, *oleracea,* is from the Latin word for potherb. Some sources suggest the name *Portulaca* means "to carry milk" and is a reference to milky sap, but this is false. If the plant looks like purslane and contains milky sap, it's spurge, a poisonous look-alike (see below).

Purslane has long been part of the human diet. In the fourth century BC, Theophrastus listed purslane as an herb to be sown in summer, and archaeologists have found seeds in the Mediterranean dating to the seventh century BC. Native to Persia, Africa, and India, it was introduced to Europe by Arabs in the 15th century as a salad herb. Most historians believe it spread to the Americas with European colonization, but some scientists now theorize that at least some species may be native to North America. More recently, purslane was listed as one of Mahatma Gandhi's favorite foods and was enjoyed by Henry David Thoreau while he lived at Walden Pond.

Currently, approximately 40 varieties of purslane are in cultivation. Although the United States lists it as the seventh most pervasive and problematic weed in the world, it's eaten as a leafy vegetable throughout much of Europe, the Middle East, Asia, Mexico, and Australia. Greeks sauté the leaves and stems with feta cheese, tomato, onion, garlic, oregano, and olive oil. Turks use it in salads, in baked pastries, and as a cooked green. Japanese use it as part of a traditional dish served during the Japanese new year. Australian Aborigines use the seeds to make seedcakes.

You could say that purslane comes in two flavors: sweet and sour. At night, purslane leaves trap carbon dioxide, which is converted into malic acid. During the daylight hours, the malic acid is converted into glucose. When harvested in the early morning, the leaves have as much as 10 times the malic acid content as those harvested in the late afternoon, giving them a much tangier, sour flavor.

In addition to its food value, purslane has a long history of use by herbalists for a variety of ailments. Ancients considered its healing properties so reliable they wore it in amulets to ward off evil. Today, herbalists use purslane to treat ailments including cardiac weakness, dry cough, diarrhea, dysentery, fever, gingivitis, high cholesterol, hypertension, sore throat, urinary tract infections, bee stings, boils, burns, and hemorrhoids. Purslane is known as Ma Chi Xian ("horse tooth amaranth") in traditional Chinese medicine.

Purslane is a well-known beneficial weed in organic farming. As a companion plant, it provides a ground cover or natural mulch, stabilizing soil moisture. In addition, its deep roots bring up moisture and nutrients, making them available to other plants with shallower roots. Some plant roots tag along with purslane's through hard soil that they would otherwise be unable to penetrate.

IN THE FIELD

What It Looks Like: Stems thick, smooth, branched, reddish, 4–10 inches long, succulent (water filled). Leaves green, alternate or opposite, paddle- or spoon-shaped, ½–2 inches long, succulent. In late summer and fall, very small (⅛- to ¼-inch-wide) yellow, five-petaled flowers bloom from between base of leaf and stem. Flowers open for only a few hours on sunny mornings; blooms stay closed on overcast days. After pollination, flower's base enlarges to become a capsule containing tiny black seeds. It self-sows freely. Taproot with fibrous secondary roots is able to penetrate dry, compacted soils. A tenacious survivor in many conditions, but not frost hardy.

Where to Find: Occurs throughout the United States. From late spring to fall on sunny lawns and meadows, but also grows in partial shade. Often thrives in cracks of sunny sidewalks and driveways. Also common in container gardens, flower beds, gardens, fields, waste ground, and roadsides. An excellent plant for rooftop gardens. Prefers rich, moist, well-drained soil located in full sun. Easily transplanted to a container and brought indoors to winter over.

When to Harvest: June through October. Depending upon rainfall, flowers appear at any time during the year. Leaves harvested during morning hours are tangier than those collected in the afternoon.

What to Eat: Leaves, stems, flower buds, flowers.

How to Harvest: Gently lift the stem and leaves from the surface they're growing over, then break or snip the stem at the ground.

Poisonous Look-Alikes to Avoid: Several low-growing spurges (*Euphorbia* spp.) share characteristics with purslane, but they are easily distinguished by thinner leaves and milky sap. Purslane has thickened leaves and lacks milky sap. See Petty Spurge in chapter 6.

IN THE KITCHEN

Why You Should Eat It: Contains more omega-3 fatty acid than any other green leafy plant. A single cup contains about 350 milligrams of this essential fatty acid. In addition, it contains respectable levels of vitamin C, vitamin A, calcium, magnesium, potassium, and iron. It also contains a red pigment, betacyanin, and a yellow pigment, betaxanthin, both of which are potent antioxidants.

Who Should Avoid It: Contains oxalic acid, a concern for people with urinary tract and/or kidney problems (see Oxalic Acid sidebar in this chapter).

What It Tastes Like: Pleasantly crunchy, refreshing, moist, with a mildly sweet-sour flavor. Leaves harvested during morning hours are tangier than those collected in the afternoon. No bitter taste. Slightly mucilaginous.

How to Store: Rinse in cool water and drain on a soft cloth. Refrigerate in an airtight container with a damp paper towel for up to four days.

How to Cook: Stems and leaves are good in salads, soups, stir-fries, and sautés. Sprinkle leaves over any dish that would benefit from a lemony zing. Use chopped purslane as a thickening agent in place of okra. Stems are often pickled; to clean, use a sharp knife to trim tough stems near the roots. Grind dried seeds just before use and add to flour.

Purslane Greek Salad

Greek salad presents so many distinct flavors: pungent feta cheese, salty kalamata olives, sweet bell peppers. Why not incorporate the unexpected for a change? Purslane's lemony crunch adds another layer of complexity to this salad.

* SERVES 4 TO 6 *

VINAIGRETTE

2 cloves garlic, minced

1 teaspoon fresh oregano

½ teaspoon Dijon mustard

¼ cup good red wine vinegar

1 teaspoon kosher salt

½ teaspoon freshly ground black pepper

½ cup extra virgin olive oil

SALAD

1 English cucumber, unpeeled and sliced ¼ inch thick

1 red bell pepper, diced

1 yellow bell pepper, diced

1 pint cherry tomatoes, halved

½ red onion, sliced very thinly in half-rounds

1 cup purslane leaves, stems removed

½ pound feta cheese, coarsely crumbled

½ cup pitted kalamata olives

Whisk together all vinaigrette ingredients except for the oil. Still whisking briskly and continuously, slowly add the olive oil to make an emulsion.

Place the cucumber, peppers, tomatoes, red onion, and purslane in a large salad bowl. Pour the vinaigrette over the vegetables and gently toss. Add the feta cheese and olives and gently toss once or twice more. Cover and set aside for 30 minutes to allow the flavors to blend. Serve at room temperature.

Purslane and Caper Salad

A wonderfully refreshing summer side dish, this salad is just as delicious in the winter. My recipe is based on a traditional Cretan salad. If my lawn weeds are abundant, I like to add a cup each of cat's ear and dandelion greens.

* SERVES 4 *

1 cup canned chickpeas, drained

2 teaspoons pickled capers

10 pitted whole kalamata olives

2 cloves garlic, finely chopped

¼ red onion, thinly sliced

2 tablespoons extra virgin olive oil, or as needed

2 tablespoons fresh lemon juice, or as needed

Salt and pepper to taste

1½ cups arugula leaves, torn into pieces

¾ cup purslane leaves, stems removed

In a large mixing bowl, combine chickpeas, capers, olives, garlic, and red onion. Add olive oil and lemon juice. Mix well, and season to taste.

Toss in arugula and purslane. Serve immediately.

Sheep Sorrel

Red Sorrel, Sour Weed, Field Sorrel
Rumex acetosella (synonym *Acetosella vulgaris*)

What is it about kids and sour treats? Today we have Sourpatch Kids candy. In my day it was Pixy Stix, Sweet Tarts, and Jolly Rancher candy. It should come as no surprise then that all kids seem to love sheep sorrel. It is among the first plants children taste test on their own. Perhaps the shimmery leaves draw their attention first, then once they taste a leaf, they are sold. I too enjoyed a nibble as a child but "unlearned" the plant's edibility as I became a young adult and had to rediscover it through books like the one you're reading.

Sheep sorrel is an herbaceous perennial in the Polygonaceae (buckwheat) family. The plant is native to Eurasia but has been introduced to most of the rest of the northern hemisphere. The word sorrel comes from the French word for "sour."

Though most of us tend to ignore the lowly wild variety, many gardeners labor to grow a larger, less flavorful variety, the garden sorrel, *Rumex acetosa*, is considered a gourmet vegetable. In the United States, sheep sorrel is widely considered to be a noxious weed. It is difficult to control due to its spreading rhizome. Farmers often see it as a message to apply lime since its presence indicates acidic soils.

IN THE FIELD

What It Looks Like: Upright, slender, reddish stem; individual stems branched near the top and generally grow 4–12 inches tall, but in ideal growing conditions may reach heights of 18–20 inches. Arrow- or spade-shaped leaves make the plant one of the easiest to identify. Leaves green, succulent, and slightly more than an inch in length, with a smooth pair of horizontal lobes at base. Most leaves have a slight shimmer when held in the sun. Male flowers yellowish-green; female flowers, developing on separate plants, red to maroon. Fruits are red achenes. Seeds reddish or golden brown with rust-brown hulls; can remain viable in soil for 10–20 years. Shallow, fibrous roots and extensive horizontal roots can reach depths of 5 feet. Reproduces by seeds and by creeping roots that produce new shoots.

Where to Find: Occurs throughout the United States on lawns, meadows, fields, grasslands, and woodlands. Favors moist soil; thrives in floodplains and near marshes. Often one of the first species to take hold in disturbed areas, especially if soil is acidic. Does well in sunny sites that are sparsely vegetated, especially where soils are sand or gravel. Although it needs well-drained soil, its moisture requirements prevent it from growing in arid areas. Best places to find it are old fields on sandy soil, roadsides, gravel and sand pits, and naturally bare sites such as steep slopes, beaches, and banks.

When to Harvest: Leaves don't become tough or bitter with age, as many other greens do, and can be gathered throughout spring, summer, and fall.

What to Eat: Leaves. Stems and leaf stalks generally too tough; flowers, while edible, are small and slightly bitter.

How to Harvest: Pick leaves as you would any leafy green vegetable.

Poisonous Look-Alikes to Avoid: None.

IN THE KITCHEN

Why You Should Eat It: High in vitamins C and A, iron, and calcium.

Who Should Avoid It: Contains oxalic acid, which can

be a concern for people prone to kidney stones (see Oxalic Acid sidebar in this chapter).

What It Tastes Like: Leaves have a tangy, lemony flavor.

How to Store: Place stems in water to store leaves in refrigerator or on the counter for two or three days. Leaves in contact with water turn brown within a few hours, so fill the container with water only to cover bottoms of stems.

How to Cook: Commonly used as a tart flavoring agent for sauces, soups, and salads. Also used as a curdling agent for cheesemaking.

Sheep Sorrel and Smoked Trout Salad

You don't really need vinegar or lemon when you have sheep sorrel. I recommend a creamy dressing for this salad, however, because the sorrel can pack quite a punch of sour delight. Consider making your own ranch dressing by blending equal parts mayonnaise and buttermilk or yogurt, then seasoning to taste with fresh or dried dill and garlic powder.

* SERVES 4 *

3 cups mildly flavored greens such as
    lamb's-quarter or lettuce
1 cup sheep sorrel
1 large avocado, pitted, peeled, diced to
    ½-inch cubes
2 tablespoons ranch (or other creamy)
    dressing
12 ounces smoked trout, cut or broken into
    2-inch pieces (can substitute smoked
    salmon)

In a large salad bowl, toss greens, sheep sorrel, avocado, and dressing. Top with smoked trout and serve.

Sheep sorrel leaves look like arrows or sheep's heads: a long pointed nose and two ears.

Sheep Sorrel and Soft Goat Cheese Spread

This recipe makes a mouthwatering, creamy cheese spread, but if you are like me with your taste testing, you will wind up with somewhat less than the stated amount.

* MAKES 1¼ CUPS *

½ cup finely chopped sheep sorrel
8 ounces soft goat (or other) cheese
2 to 3 tablespoons extra virgin olive oil,
    depending on desired thickness
1 clove garlic
Sea salt and fresh ground pepper to taste

Blend all ingredients in a food processor until sheep sorrel is minced finely. Serve with crackers or crostini.

Sheep Sorrel and Soft Goat Cheese Spread is a tangy
complement to bread or crackers.

Shotweed

Bittercress, Hairy Bittercress
Cardamine hirsuta

once had a roommate who worked for a landscape maintenance company. Occasionally he needed extra help, and I would accompany him on his rounds. Usually our gardening took us to landscapes that had been repeatedly sprayed with Roundup to eliminate weeds. The Roundup treatment was effective enough on certain weeds, but not so much on others. We often encountered previously sprayed flower beds that were devoid of everything *except* for a nice hardy field of shotweed. I have to admire any plant that can outsmart the likes of Monsanto, Ortho, and Dupont.

My friend and I removed the shotweed by hand, but it seemed like a pointless exercise. Each time my fingers grazed the tops of the plants, tiny projectile seeds shot all over the place, sometimes as far as 6 or 7 feet. I decided then and there that the name "shotweed" was the most apt nomenclature in the entire plant world, not to mention a great name for a band.

I about fell over when I learned this pesky garden weed was edible! Not just edible but, in my book, at the very top of the list of delicious weeds. Shotweed tastes peppery like watercress or nasturtiums. I never bother to cook it as I don't want to lose any of its wonderful flavor.

The genus name *Cardamine* is derived from *kardamonon,* the Greek word for "cardamom," a member of the ginger family, possibly because they both have strong flavors and are used to flavor foods. The species name *hirsuta* is the Latin word for "hairy," a reference to the plant's hairy stems—thus another of its common names is "hairy bittercress."

Shotweed is an herbaceous annual imported to North America from Europe. It grows so prolifically that it's the curse of many a gardener who doesn't realize how flavorful it is. North America is also home to several native *Cardamine* species, most of which are edible, but the European species is somewhat unique in its ability to reproduce.

Though usually regarded as one of the peskiest garden weeds, shotweed is beneficial to the gardener in a number of ways. It's one of the first flowers to bloom, providing a valuable early nectar source for bees and other pollinators. Also, some gardeners use shotweed as a winter groundcover or green manure, though unless you want a continuing crop of it, take care to till it in or dig it up before it goes to seed. Finally, it's a good pest-trap crop for aphids, as they favor it over many other prone plants.

IN THE FIELD

What It Looks Like: Stems generally 3–8 inches tall, though can grow up to 18 inches depending on location. Leaves a basal rosette; each leaf comprised of smaller, round leaflets or lobes opposite each other. Terminal leaflet slightly larger than lateral leaflets. At maturity, numerous tiny, white, four-petaled flowers appear on ends of wiry, green stems. When touched even slightly, the small seed head explodes, shooting its 15–22 seeds a distance of several feet. Seeds germinate in fall, and in milder climates new plants often emerge as early as January. Small taproot is surrounded by small, fibrous rootlets.

Where to Find: Occurs throughout the United States except Colorado, Delaware, Iowa, Kansas, Maine, Minnesota, Montana, Nebraska, Nevada, New Hampshire, North Dakota, South Dakota, Utah, Vermont, Wisconsin, and Wyoming. Found in any disturbed soil, gardens, landscapes, and roadsides. Tolerates most soils, but grows best in damp, freshly disturbed soil and among rocks, scree, and walls.

When to Harvest: Late winter, spring. Greens best harvested before seeds form. If you're trying to eradicate it from your flower or vegetable garden, definitely collect it before it goes to seed! And good luck.

What to Eat: Entire plant, but roots less palatable and more difficult to clean than rest of plant.

How to Harvest: Pull entire plant up with one hand, then use other hand to twist roots off before placing plant in a bowl. This method keeps your harvest cleaner.

Poisonous Look-Alikes to Avoid: None.

IN THE KITCHEN

Why You Should Eat It: High in vitamin C; carries the many health benefits of other plants in the mustard (brassica) family.

What It Tastes Like: Delicious! Very similar to watercress or nasturtiums. Despite one of its common names, bittercress, it is not at all bitter tasting.

How to Store: Rinse well and use a salad spinner to remove excess water. Store loosely in a plastic bag in refrigerator crisper. You can also keep it fresh in a vase or a glass of water for a day or two.

How to Cook: Most delicious raw in salads and sandwiches or as a garnish. Although it retains much of its nutritional value when cooked, its peppery flavor is largely lost.

Shotweed and Pan-Seared Scallops

Consider the delectable marriage of scallops and watercress, for that is essentially what this recipe is. The difference is that shotweed's clumping nature makes a more lovely, springy cloud of greens for the scallops to float atop.

* SERVES 4 *

4 tablespoons extra virgin olive oil, divided
1 tablespoon seasoned rice vinegar
Salt and pepper to taste
4 cups loosely packed shotweed, hard stems removed
2 tablespoons ghee (clarified butter)
8 large scallops, rinsed and patted dry

In a large salad bowl, whisk 2 tablespoons olive oil with vinegar and seasonings. Add shotweed and toss. Divide equally onto four salad plates.

In a large skillet over high heat, melt ghee in remaining 2 tablespoons olive oil. Once skillet is very hot (nearly smoking), place scallops flat-side down. Do not overcrowd the pan. Once you've placed the scallops, do not move them.

After 2 minutes, use a spatula to check doneness. When undersides have a caramel-colored crust, turn the scallops. Cook another minute or so and remove from pan. (Centers should still be slightly translucent as observed from the sides.)

Place two scallops, caramel side up, over each plate of greens. Serve immediately.

Shotweed Salad

If you aren't able to find enough shotweed to comprise an entire salad (unlikely), you can certainly add other greens. But the flavor is excellent all on its own and needs no accompaniment. And if you're like me and on a diet half the time, you'll appreciate that this salad doesn't even require a dressing.

* SERVES 4 *

3 cups shotweed, loosely packed

2 tablespoons balsamic vinegar

Juice of 1 lime

1 teaspoon honey

3 tablespoons extra virgin olive oil

1 tablespoon finely grated or minced sweet
   onion (Vidalia or Walla Walla)

1 firm, ripe avocado, diced to to ½-inch cubes

2 tablespoons crumbled cooked bacon

Rinse and dry shotweed, removing any tough stems. In a large salad bowl, whisk together vinegar, lime juice, honey, olive oil, and onion. Add avocado and shotweed to vinegar mixture and toss. Sprinkle bacon over the salad and serve.

As shotweed goes to seed, the stems become tough and unpalatable.

Sweet Briar Rose

Eglantine Rose

Rosa rubiginosa, Rosa eglanteria, or *Rosa mosqueta*

When I was ten, we moved to a commune near Eugene, Oregon. (Yes, you are probably right: this is likely when and where my latent hippy seed was planted.) My mother decided it wasn't for her, so we weren't there for very long, but, short visit that it was, it was a very memorable time for me. Every night, two kids my age climbed up a handmade ladder to sleep in a loft in their family's A-frame. At the time, I didn't think it got any more awesome than that. I very much wanted a loft of my own. (Maybe someday—I'm a firm believer that it's never too late for anything.)

Another thing they did that was ultracool to my 10-year-old mind was to store all kinds of dried wild edible things in canning jars. I didn't eat much from their pantry, but I remember that visually it was quite pleasing, and I enjoyed looking at the variety of colors and shapes. I stayed overnight with my new friends up in their loft a few times. Each morning as part of breakfast, their mother would hand out our vitamin C "pills": dried rose hips. I chewed mine up and spit the seeds out as instructed, all the while thinking to myself that this was a far superior way to take one's morning vitamins than in pill form.

After we moved back into our "normal" house, I kept my own small jar of rose hips. Except now I didn't think of them as medicine so much as a sort of candy. They were sweet and sour, reminding me of lollipops, and were just good to have on hand as a small snack.

For this book, I chose the sweet briar rose because it is common in many settings, but all roses have edible hips, young leaves, and flowers and may be substituted in my recipes. In general, a rose is a woody perennial in the genus *Rosa,* of the family Rosaceae. The genus includes well over 100 species and, because they hybridize easily, today there is an astonishingly wide range of thousands of hybrids and cultivars worldwide. Most species are native to Asia, with a relative few indigenous to Europe, North America, and Africa. Rose flowers come in colors ranging from white to yellow to red to purple and are often large and showy. Rose hips are the edible red fruits left behind after the bloom has died. All rose hips are edible, though some contain higher levels of vitamin C than others. As members of the apple family, some roses produce very large hips. For example, *Rosa rugosa,* a rose often used in landscapes, produces hips that are as big as crab apples. Petals and young leaves are also edible.

The sweet briar rose is native to Europe and western Asia. The name eglantine derives from Latin *aculeatus* ("thorny"), by way of old French *aiglant.* Sweet refers to the apple fragrance of the foliage, while briar (also sometimes spelled "brier") is an old Anglo-Saxon word for any thorny shrub.

Roses have been used in herbal and folk medicines for millennia. Chinese traditional medicine uses rose hips to treat stomach problems. Scientists are now studying them for controlling cancer growth.

In addition to its pink flowers, sweet briar rose is highly valued for its scent and flavorful hips that persist well into winter. In Tunisia, natural flower water is produced from its flowers. In Chile and Argentina, the hips are cultivated for marmalades and cosmetic products. Rich in carotenoids, sweet briar rose hips are being studied in Spain and elsewhere in Europe for their use in food colorings, vitamin A supplements, and skin and scalp restoratives.

In fact, you can now pay $30 to $50 for an ounce of eglantine rose skin and scalp restorative advertised thus:

"extracted from a rose that grows high in Chile's Andes Mountains, a little of this rich oil goes a long way to nourish and revitalize dull, dry skin." Or grow your own to produce skin products for free in your own kitchen.

A century ago, sweet briar rose was a common feature in the flower garden. It eventually fell from favor as people's preferences turned toward hybrids with showier blooms. However, over the past few decades, rose aficionados have once again begun turning to the "old fashioned" roses as garden favorites, and R. *rubiginosa* can once again be found in many nurseries.

IN THE FIELD

What It Looks Like: Dense deciduous shrub 6–9 feet high and across; stems bear numerous hooked prickles. While we usually refer to roses as having thorns, sharp protrusions along rose stems are actually outgrowths of the epidermis (outer layer of stem tissue) called prickles (true thorns are modified stems always originating at a node). Rose prickles are generally curved hooks used to hang onto other vegetation as the rose plant grows over it. Despite these prickles, roses are frequently browsed by deer. Foliage has a strong applelike fragrance. Leaves pinnate, 2–4 inches long, with five to nine rounded to oval leaflets with a serrated margin and numerous glandular hairs. Flowers fragrant, ¾–1¼ inches in diameter, with five pink petals paler toward the base. Numerous yellow stamens. Flowers produced in clusters of two to seven from late spring through midsummer. Fruit a round to oblong red hip, growing to 1½ inches in diameter. R. *rubiginosa* hips are one of the tastier varieties. Rosehips have an outer fleshy layer (the edible part) called the hypanthium, which contains 5–160 achenes (fruits) held in a fine web of stiff hairs. Each achene contains a single seed. Seeds are dispersed in droppings of fruit-eating birds such as thrushes and waxwings.

Where to Find: Throughout much of Canada and most of the United States, except Arizona, Florida, Hawaii, Louisiana, Nevada, New Mexico, North Dakota, and South Dakota. This species grows well in either full sun or partial shade. Though it prefers moist sites and is often found growing along roadside ditches and river banks, sweet briar rose tolerates a wide variety of soils and growing conditions, even surviving floods and long periods of drought.

When to Harvest: Gather petals, shoots, and leaves any time they are present. Rose hips begin to form in spring and ripen in late summer through autumn; harvest hips after first frost when they are fully colored but not overripe. Best when they yield to gentle pressure but are also quite fine after they've shriveled and become soft. If you pick rose hips a little early, place them in the freezer for a few hours to imitate a frost. In late summer and early autumn, plants often bear fruit and flowers at the same time.

What to Eat: Rose hips, petals, young shoots, young leaves.

How to Harvest: Be careful of prickles; wear long sleeves, long pants, and gloves, but note that dexterity is greatly reduced by wearing gloves. If I see a good bush, I pick regardless of what I am wearing. Make sure rose petals you're going to use are pesticide free.

Poisonous Look-Alikes to Avoid: None.

IN THE KITCHEN

Why You Should Eat It: Rose hips contain high levels of lycopene, an antioxidant that helps to control cholesterol. Rose hips also contain high levels of vitamin A and antioxidant flavonoids. A study of a rose hip supplement concluded there is a benefit to those with rheumatoid arthritis due to both its anti-inflammatory and antioxidant effects. Rose hips, incredibly high in vitamin C, are also often used to help prevent and treat colds and influenza.

What It Tastes Like: Rose hips are fruity and spicy, not unlike a cranberry.

How to Store: Fully dry petals, hips, and leaves and store in airtight containers. Hips and petals can also be preserved by canning.

How to Cook: Sprinkle petals raw on salads, use raw as a garnish, candy them, or make into rose petal jelly; wash them thoroughly first. Use rose hips for herbal tea, jam, jelly, syrup, soup, beverages, pies, bread, wine, chutney, and marmalade. They can also be eaten raw, like a berry, if care is used to avoid swallowing the hairs inside the hip. Recipes for both hips and petals are abundant on the internet; most recipes advise removing the seeds. When cooking with rose hips, use stainless steel or other non-reactive containers to avoid discoloring of the fruit and loss of vitamin C. Eat young shoots raw or cooked. Cook young leaves to reduce or remove toughness and hairiness.

Sweet Briar Rose Hip Nut Bread

This bread is so wonderfully earthy, it may very well have been invented at the commune I mentioned above. Sweet, moist, and aromatic, it makes a wonderful breakfast treat. Rosehip nut bread is a traditional American recipe from Alaska.

* MAKES ONE LOAF *

Juice of 1 orange, plus water to make 1 cup
½ cup chopped raisins
¾ cup seeded and chopped sweet briar
   rose hips
2 tablespoons melted butter
1 teaspoon vanilla
1 egg, beaten
1½ cups flour
1 cup sugar
1 teaspoon baking powder
½ teaspoon baking soda
¼ teaspoon salt
½ cup nuts or sunflower seeds

Preheat oven to 350°F. In a large bowl, mix orange juice, raisins, rose hips, butter, vanilla, and egg. Separately, sift together the dry ingredients and then add to first mixture. Mix just until ingredients are combined; do not overmix. Gently stir in nuts or sunflower seeds. Pour or spoon batter into a well-greased 5-by-8-inch loaf pan and bake for one hour.

Rose Petal Ice Cubes

This is a simply beautiful way to serve rose petals. The frozen delicacies are lovely in a glass of fruit juice or punch. Also, this is one of those easy, relatively nonmessy kitchen activities that your young children will enjoy.

* MAKES 12 TO 24 ICE CUBES *

15–20 small rose petals
water
ice cube tray(s)

Choose petals that are small because they are easier to fit into ice cube trays; wash them thoroughly.

Boil water for about two minutes to let air trapped in the water escape. This step ensures that the rose petal ice cubes will be crystal clear. Let water cool to room temperature.

Fill ice cube tray halfway with this cooled water. Place a rose petal in the center of each cube; the petals may float to the surface, but don't worry. Freeze the tray. After the water freezes, take the tray out and fill it again with water to cover the rose petals, then refreeze it.

Like most kids, my friend Odin enjoys making Rose Petal Ice Cubes. *(Photo by Melleoux d'Estrés)*

I'm so hungry, I could eat a tree

The well-known naturalist Euell Gibbons reminded us that "many parts [of a pine tree] are edible." Here is a short list of some common trees with edible parts. (For more information, see Linda Runyon's *Eat the Trees!*)

BLOSSOMS

Apple

Citrus (oranges, lemons, limes, grapefruit, etc.)

Dogwood

Hawthorn

Maple

Peach

Pear

FRUITS OR NUTS

Arbutus

Dogwood

Hawthorn

Pine

CATKINS AND POLLEN

Male catkins, which are high in protein during winter, are nutty tasting. Even when they're falling apart, they can be dried and ground into flour. They can also be used raw or cooked, but avoid the female woody cones.

Alder

Birch

Hazel

LEAVES

These leaves can be eaten raw or cooked, or dried and ground into flour.

Birch

Cottonwood

Dogwood

Elm

Fir

Hawthorn

Maple

Pine

Poplar

Spruce

Willow

CAMBIUM

The cambium of many trees is also edible—and palatable! Cambium is the tender inner layer of bark just beneath the hard outer bark. Using a knife, collect a couple 6-inch strips of bark from several young trees, then scrape the cambium into a container. Never collect cambium in continuous strips around the tree trunk (girdling), as this will kill the tree. Cambium is at its best when collected low on the plant during late spring and early summer. Cambium can be eaten raw, steamed, boiled, fried, roasted, or dried and ground into flour. Pine cambium is considered the choicest, but other trees also have edible cambium.

Alder

Aspen

Birch

Cottonwood

Fir

Hemlock

Larch

Linden

Maple

Oak

Pine

Poplar

Western red cedar

4 | PARKS AND GREENBELTS

Many urban park lawns are bordered by lush stands of wild, weedy plants. Greenbelts, urban areas intentionally left natural and undeveloped, are also prime locations for finding a variety of edible weeds.

I especially enjoy collecting from these areas as it's a great opportunity to teach others about urban foraging. I see it as a dual mission because, without fail, I have a number of people approach me to ask what I'm collecting and why. The response I get is typically one of delight mixed with wonder. "I never knew you could eat that plant! My mom always told me it was poisonous!"

Before collecting plants from parks and other public spaces like greenbelts, be sure you're allowed to do so legally and that you are collecting from an area free of pesticides. Usually, a quick call to the city parks department will provide you with answers.

Note that while these weeds are common to park and greenbelt edges and borders, they are often found in many other urban spaces too.

Bedstraw

Cleavers, Catchweed
Galium aparine

've long been familiar with this plant, having learned in ethnobotany about its early Native American use as bedding. It's true, bedstraw is light and airy and smells quite sweet when it's dried.

Years later, when I discovered it was edible, I had the bedding association so firmly planted in my mind that I couldn't bring myself to take a bite, and it was a number of years before I worked up the nerve to sample it. As is sometimes the case, my first attempt did not go too well. I decided to boil several large handfuls of it, which resulted in a pot full of coarse, brambly, strawlike greens. Apparently, I'd gathered from plants that were well past their prime, and they were already impregnated with silica, something that happens with bedstraw. I learned that to enjoy it, you have to harvest bedstraw early in the spring when it is very young and tender, ideally no higher than 8 inches.

The second time I tried it, I sampled a much younger sprig in the raw. It had a clean, sweet flavor a bit like sugar peas, and I was an immediate convert. Now I look forward every February and March to that two- or three-week window when I can harvest it for an early spring salad.

Bedstraw is an herbaceous annual plant native to North America and Eurasia. The word *galium* is from *gala,* which is Greek for "milk." It was so named because in parts of Europe it was traditionally used to strain milk. In addition, the plant contains a milk-curdling enzyme historically used in cheese making. The flowering tops, yellow with a honeylike fragrance, were used for coloring and scenting cheese and butter. In Jewish American communities and in Israel, it is still sometimes used for making kosher cheeses. The fruits were used by Belgian lace-makers as heads for their pins.

Bedstraw is related to the coffee plant, and its seeds can be used to make an excellent coffee substitute simply by drying and lightly roasting them. In fact, if you eat bread or cereal, you've already been eating bedstraw seeds. The plant is a common weed in grain crops, and its seeds are difficult to remove during processing.

IN THE FIELD

What It Looks Like: Long, rambling stems (up to 6 feet long or more) run along hedges and edges of landscapes. Six to eight leaves form a whorl around a square stem. Leaves and stems have fine hairs tipped with tiny hooks, making them cling to clothes and fur much like Velcro. Flowers tiny and white, with four petals, growing in whorls of six to eight at leaf nodes. In late summer and fall, fruits are clustered one to three seeds together; each seed is a burr about ⅛–¼ inch in diameter covered with hooked hairs that cling to animal fur (and your socks), aiding in seed dispersal.

Where to Find: Occurs throughout the United States except Hawaii. Commonly found among other low vegetation, especially along hedges, as well as in fields and gardens. As it grows, bedstraw forms thick, tangled mats, shading other smaller plants.

When to Harvest: When very young and no more than 8 inches tall, before it flowers in March through June. Older leaves become impregnated with silica, making them too tough to be used as food. Gather seeds in late summer and autumn.

What to Eat: Stems, leaves, seeds.

How to Harvest: Remove plant easily from soil with a single tug, or leave roots intact and just take top third to

half of the plant. Gather seeds by walking through a patch of bedstraw while wearing thick woolen socks. Seriously.
Poisonous Look-Alikes to Avoid: None.

IN THE KITCHEN

Why You Should Eat It: Rich in vitamin C.

What It Tastes Like: Raw or cooked, young bedstraw is reminiscent of sugar peas.

How to Store: Like lettuce; store leaves in a loose plastic bag in refrigerator vegetable crisper drawer (see Storing Urban Weeds sidebar in chapter 1). Lightly roast, dry, and store seeds like coffee.

How to Cook: Cook the leaves and stems as a leaf vegetable before blossoms appear. Dry, roast, and grind fruits to brew as a coffee substitute.

Bedstraw is also called "cleaver" because the seeds "cleave" to hair and clothing like Velcro.

Bedstraw, Shiitake Mushrooms, and Leeks with Soba Noodles

Most Japanese soba noodles are made from whole buckwheat flour (soba-ko) and whole wheat flour and are about the thickness of Italian spaghetti noodles. Soba noodles are a frequent ingredient in both hot and cold Japanese dishes. I love this meal because it's very simple to prepare and versatile enough to add any combination of vegetables. Adding chopped bedstraw to the mix makes for a colorful, healthy, and delicious meal.

* SERVES 2 TO 4 *

2 packages (8–9 ounces) soba (buckwheat) noodles
3 cups bedstraw, chopped to 1 inch
3 tablespoons olive oil
2 leeks, halved lengthwise, sliced thinly (discard top third of each leek)
½ pound fresh shiitake mushrooms, sliced (discard tough stems)
4 scallions, coarsely chopped
2 tablespoons soy sauce (or to taste)
2 tablespoons rice vinegar (or to taste)

In a medium-size pan, bring 3 cups water to a boil. Add soba and bedstraw. Cook for 5 minutes. Drain.

In a large skillet, heat olive oil over medium-high heat and cook leeks, stirring frequently, until softened. Add mushrooms and scallions and cook another 2–3 minutes. Add drained bedstraw, soba noodles, soy sauce, and vinegar. Toss and cook 30 seconds. May be served warm or as a cold salad.

Bedstraw Lentil Curry

Cooked lentils are one of my favorite comfort foods and a great way to increase my protein intake. But as an incomplete protein, lentils don't provide all of the essential amino acids you need. That can be remedied by combining lentils with grains. Here, serving lentils with barley is an easy, delicious way to get complete protein in a vegetarian dish. Adding bedstraw as a leafy green vegetable makes this dish nutritionally complete.

* SERVES 4 *

4 tablespoons olive oil, divided
1 medium onion, finely chopped
3 cloves garlic, minced
1 teaspoon paprika
2 teaspoons curry powder
1 teaspoon salt
2 cups water
1 cup chicken or vegetable broth
2 cups young bedstraw stems and leaves, chopped to 1-inch lengths
1½ cups red lentils

In a large frying pan, heat 2 tablespoons olive oil over medium-high heat and sauté onions and garlic. Add paprika, curry powder, and salt. Add water and broth and bring to a boil. Add bedstraw and lentils. Return to a boil. Reduce heat and simmer over low for 10 minutes or until water has been absorbed and lentils are soft. Add 2 tablespoons olive oil. Combine well. (Lentils may lose their shape.) Serve over a bed of cooked barley (or rice or wheat berries).

Horsetail

Common Horsetail, Field Horsetail, Scouring Brush
Equisetum arvense

Can you think back to the first time you ever saw horsetail? I mean really *saw* it. They are an odd standout in the plant kingdom. I'm not sure that I remember my first actual sighting, but I definitely recall the first time I picked one to inspect it. I was and still am struck by their unusual construction. They are stiff as wire, have stems with water-filled segments, have "leaves" in equidistant circles around the stems, and are beautifully symmetrical. They look like something straight out of a Dr. Seuss book!

Believed to be one of Earth's earliest ferns, *Equisetum* is the only living genus in the family Equisetaceae and the only surviving plant from the Paleozoic era. This plant is literally a living fossil, with a history dating back at least 30 million years. *Equisetum* is an herbaceous perennial, either dying back in winter in temperate regions or growing year-round in the tropics. *Equisetum* is found nearly everywhere on the globe with the exception of Antarctica.

The common name horsetail was likely assigned due to the mature plant's tail-like appearance. *Equisetum* is the only group of vascular plants that reproduce by spores rather than seeds. Size is the primary difference between *Equisetum* from the Paleozoic era and today's *Equisetum*. In Paleozoic forests, the genus was far more diverse, with some growing up to 80 feet tall. Our tallest horsetails today can be found in the tropics growing to a height of 30 feet.

Horsetail is a plant with a history of many uses. In Germany it is referred to as *Zinnkraut* or "tin herb" because it was used to polish metals. In Japanese woodworking, one species is boiled and dried for final wood burnishing. Whitesmiths, craftsmen who finished forged metals, called horsetail "pewterwort." The people of ancient Rome used a tisane of the plant to make a thickening agent; the Japanese continue to cook the shoots. Indians of the North American Pacific Northwest ate the young shoots raw and used mature plants to burnish hand tools. The leaves can be used as a light green dye.

Today horsetail has numerous medicinal uses, and an extract of the plant is often used in silica supplements. Mature plants contain so much silica that when burned in a hot flame, their ashy skeletons remain intact. Today, they continue to be used to estimate gold concentrations in soils due to their ability to absorb the dissolved precious metal.

Because horsetail is extremely resistant to fungus growth, some use it to subdue mold and fungus infections in cultivated plants. Organic farmers spray horsetail tea to rid fruit trees of leaf curl.

IN THE FIELD

What It Looks Like: Stems green, hollow, jointed. Leaves might seem to be fernlike foliage, but these are actually small branches of main stem. Branches constructed just like stems but smaller and more fragile. Leaves brown, papery, toothed sheaths around each joint or node of main stem. Stems easily broken at nodes. Roots deep rhizomes with tubers. Sterile adult plants feature whorls of branches (fernlike foliage) at nodes. Adult fertile plants lack branches, are topped by large strobilus (see photo in color section).

Where to Find: Occurs throughout the United States except Florida, Hawaii, and Louisiana. Able to grow in a wide variety of soils and conditions, but generally does not thrive in high pH soils. Commonly found in open fields, arable land, waste places, roadsides.

When to Harvest: Harvest young shoots from sterile plants in spring before they branch. Fertile shoots can also be collected and used, but they tend to be watery and flavorless.

What to Eat: Young shoots with papery sheaths removed. Roots also edible but tedious to gather; considered an emergency food.

How to Harvest: Grasp base of plant and pull upward.

Poisonous Look-Alikes to Avoid: None.

IN THE KITCHEN

Why You Should Eat It: Rich in antioxidants.

Who Should Avoid It: Frequent large quantities can be toxic because it contains thiaminase, which can rob the body of vitamin B. Thiaminase is destroyed by cooking or thoroughly drying horsetail. Horsetail takes up heavy metals and chemicals from soil, so don't gather it from roadsides or polluted locations.

What It Tastes Like: Very little flavor; takes on flavor of other ingredients in a dish. Due to its similar shape, it can be used as a mildly flavored asparagus substitute.

How to Store: Soon after harvesting, while stems are still firm, remove leaves (brown sheaths at each node). Store prepared stems for a day or two in refrigerator between damp paper towels in a closed container. Expect some browning at nodes as well as some loss of firmness, which is not noticeable after cooking. Dry horsetail shoots for a tea.

How to Cook: Eat raw, steamed, sautéed, or stir-fried. Use as a very mild-flavored asparagus substitute. Japanese cook with the fertile plant's strobilus, but steps must be taken to remove toxins prior to eating—not recommended unless you are certain you are able to remove toxins to a safe level.

Horsetail Thai-Style

Horsetail shoots take up just about any flavor you cook them with. The Japanese still frequently cook with horsetail shoots. By adding fish sauce and chile peppers, I've given this basic dish a Thai twist. For a creamier version, omit the fish sauce and sesame seed oil and add ½ cup coconut milk.

* SERVES 4 *

½ pound 8- to 12-inch-long horsetail shoots
2 tablespoons olive oil
1 teaspoon fish sauce
1 tablespoon soy or tamari sauce
1 tablespoon toasted sesame seed oil
½ teaspoon crushed red chile peppers

In a medium skillet over high heat, sauté horsetail shoots in olive oil until softened, about 5 minutes. Add fish sauce and soy sauce. Toss until stalks are coated. Add sesame seed oil and chile peppers and cook another minute. Serve immediately.

It's not hard to see how horsetail got its common name.

Horsetail with Garlic, Butter, and Thyme

I've said it before and I'm very certain I'll say it again: nearly any savory dish is improved with garlic and butter. Horsetail is fine on its own, but adding these familiar flavors for first-time diners might be just the thing to tip them toward the wonderful world of edible weeds.

* SERVES 4 *

4 tablespoons butter
3 cloves garlic, thinly sliced
½ pound horsetail shoots, outer fringes removed
1 tablespoon coarsely chopped fresh thyme
Salt and pepper to taste

In a medium skillet, melt butter over medium heat. Add garlic and sauté until golden. Add horsetail stalks and sauté 5–10 minutes, until softened, but still somewhat firm. Add thyme, salt, and pepper and cook another minute. Serve immediately.

Harvest horsetail shoots before the "tail" begins to emerge.

Linden

Large-Leaved Linden, Basswood, Bass Tree, Lime Tree, Tilia
Tilia platyphyllos

Quite honestly, I didn't even know what a linden tree was until I started writing this book. But when I saw how many culinary uses it has and how popular it seems to be with urban arborists, I had to include it.

Though I was unfamiliar with the tree, I did have some linden flower tea I brought back from Mexico, a tea that I like very much. How wonderful to learn that there is a linden-lined street just blocks from where I live! To shorten that distance to a few paces, and to provide some welcome shade, I've decided to grow one in my yard. But enough about my front yard; let's talk about the tree!

Tilia is a genus of about 30 species of deciduous trees native throughout most of the temperate northern hemisphere. In Britain, they're referred to as lime trees, but in the United States they're known as linden or basswood. Until fairly recently, this genus belonged to the family Tiliaceae. However, recent genetic research has placed it into the Malvaceae family. Most of the information for large-leaved tilia, *Tilia platyphyllos,* also applies to little-leaved linden, *Tilia cordata.* The common name basswood originates from the inner fibrous bark of the tree, known as bast. The genus name *Tilia* is of unknown origin, but some etymologists believe it may share a history with today's word "till" because the roots are effective at breaking up tight soil formations.

Although *Tilia* is native to Asia, Europe, and eastern North America, it is used as a landscaping plant in large cities all over the world. Because linden flowers are very aromatic, many 19th-century city planners called for planting the trees to mask the odors from horses and sewers. It's no wonder then that the flowers are still used to make perfumes.

Linden is a source of food almost year-round due to the fact that, except for the roots and outer bark, the entire tree is edible. There are numerous references to its use in older European recipes. Bees are highly attracted to the flowers, and lindens are reputed to produce some of the best honey in the world. Its light, sweet flavor is said to have antiseptic and calming qualities. Linden honey is more commonly produced in Eastern Europe, but it can be found online or at specialty stores in the United States.

Linden trees have many different uses. They can reach more than 100 feet in height, and many people plant them for shade, though their roots can wreak havoc with sewer pipes, sidewalks, and streets. The wood (also called basswood) is excellent for turning and carving and is used for making woodenware such as spoons, salad bowls, toys, and furniture. During the Anglo-Saxon era, linden wood was prized for making shields. Linden's excellent acoustic properties make it a popular wood for guitars, wind instruments, and drum shells. Linden bark forms long strings that can be peeled off and braided for cordage; Native Americans used it to make baskets, containers, and rope. The inner bark is used by the Ainu people of Japan to weave traditional clothing.

Herbalists credit linden flowers with many medicinal properties, among them relief from colds, coughs, fever, infection, inflammation, high blood pressure, and headache (particularly migraine) and as a diuretic, antispasmodic, and sedative. Charcoal from the twigs and inner bark was widely used in much the same way charcoal pills are today, to absorb toxins or intestinal gas and to treat diarrhea.

What It Looks Like: Grows to more than 100 feet tall with foliage canopy more than 40 feet wide, sometimes living for many centuries. On young trees, fine bark smooth and gray-green; bark of mature trees becomes gray to brown with long, shallow furrows and flat-topped ridges. Leaves alternate, simple, unevenly ovate to cordate, 1–5 inches long, with serrated edges. Flowers pale yellow, borne in 2- to 4-inch clusters below a pale green modified leaf that looks like a long, narrow wing. Beginning when tree is about 15 years old, fall fruits born in clusters of round, smooth nutlets, about ¼ inch diameter, first green in color, then covered with gray-brown hairs at maturity. Older trees as well as stumps sucker prolifically from the base.

Where to Find: Occurs throughout the United States in parks, landscapes, along streets and sidewalks. Does well in slightly acidic soils that drain well but tolerates many soil conditions. Tolerates many climates but not drought tolerant for long periods.

When to Harvest: Young leaves in April and May; older leaves May through September. Flowers in June and July. Small nuts throughout fall and into winter.

What to Eat: Flowers, leaf buds, leaves, sap, nuts, cambium.

Young linden leaves are tender, nearly translucent, and make a delicious salad green.

How to Harvest: Many lindens produce suckers low on the trunk each spring, making for an easy harvest with a garden snips. In the absence of suckers, a ladder is probably necessary as lowest limbs are often out of reach on older, taller trees.

Poisonous Look-Alikes to Avoid: None.

IN THE KITCHEN

Why You Should Eat It: Leaves high in calcium, magnesium, nitrogen, and potassium. Linden leaf flour beneficial when added to wheat flour as it contains a high percentage of invert sugars and can be readily metabolized by diabetics.

Who Should Avoid It: Some sources claim older flowers, when used to make strong teas, can produce symptoms of narcotic intoxication.

What It Tastes Like: Flowers sweet and fragrant. Raw leaves tender, sweet, slightly mucilaginous. Brewed sap mildly flavored and sweet. Ripe linden fruits taste very much like chocolate, so much so that they're under study as a commercial chocolate substitute.

How to Store: Keep dried leaves, nuts, flowers, or flour (see recipes) in airtight containers for up to a year. Fresh young leaves and flowers last only a day or two in refrigerator once they're picked.

How to Cook: Eat young leaves raw in salads or cooked as greens. Dry and powder older leaves for use as a flour substitute and as a thickener in soups and stews. Tap the sap and use as a refreshing drink or concentrate into a syrup for use as a sweetener. Add flowers raw to salads or dry and add to herbal teas. Make a convincing chocolate substitute from the paste of ground fruits and flowers.

Linden Leaf Pancakes

Making linden leaf flour is simple, fun, and gratifying. For just a moment, I feel like a real pioneer woman! The flour turns out beautiful emerald-green pancakes that taste faintly like the sweet smell of autumn leaves, a flavor that's surprisingly lovely.

* MAKES 8 PANCAKES *

LINDEN LEAF FLOUR

> 1 pound fresh, mature linden leaves

PANCAKES

> ¾ cup all-purpose flour
> ¾ cup linden leaf flour
> 3½ teaspoons baking powder
> 1 teaspoon salt
> 1 tablespoon granulated sugar
> 1¼ cups milk
> 1 egg
> 3 tablespoons butter, melted

To make the flour, dry the linden leaves outdoors in the summer, which may take up to a week. Alternatively, place leaves on baking sheets, well separated, and dry them in a 115°F oven for up to 24 hours; this may be done in overnight shifts so that your oven is available for other uses during the day. When leaves are completely dried and crumble between your fingers, blend or pound them to a powder with mortar and pestle or in a food processor. Sift powder through a fine-meshed sieve and discard coarser material. The resulting fine flour can be stored for a year or more in an airtight jar. Typically, each pound of fresh linden leaves yields ¾ cup flour.

To make the pancakes, in a large bowl, sift together both types of flour, baking powder, salt, and sugar.

Separately, blend together milk, egg, and melted butter. Make a shallow well in center of flour mixture and pour in liquid mixture. Mix until fairly smooth; some small lumps may remain.

Heat a lightly oiled griddle or frying pan over medium-high heat. Using a soup ladle or large spoon, pour or scoop batter onto the griddle, about ¼ cup per pancake. Brown on both sides. Serve hot.

Linden Blossom Crème Brûlée

Introducing the flavor of linden flowers to crème brûlée is simply genius but, alas, I can't personally take credit. This is actually a very traditional European recipe called Crème Brûlée au Tilleul, *a variation on that classic French dessert I once clumsily mispronounced as "kreem BROO-lee."*

* MAKES 2 TO 4 *

> 1½ cups cream
> 5 tablespoons milk
> 4 tablespoons linden blossoms (dried or fresh)
> 4 egg yolks
> ½ cup sugar
> 3 tablespoons turbinado sugar

Combine cream, milk, and linden blossoms in a saucepan and bring just to a boil. Remove from heat and set aside to infuse for 20 minutes, then strain through a fine-meshed sieve or cheesecloth.

Meanwhile, beat together egg yolks and ½ cup sugar until foamy. Slowly add strained cream mixture, beating constantly. Divide custard into two to four ramekins or ovenproof dishes.

Bring water to a boil, place brûlée dishes in a baking tin, then pour the boiling water around so it comes halfway up the sides of the dishes. Transfer to a preheated 300°F oven and bake for about one hour, or until custard is set around the edges (but still loose in the center). Cooking time depends on the ramekins you choose, but begin checking after about 35 minutes.

When done, remove from oven and set aside (still in the water bath) until completely cooled.

Once cold, remove ramekins from water bath and chill in refrigerator for at least two hours and up to two days.

Just before serving, sprinkle turbinado sugar over crème brûlées. Melt and caramelize sugar topping with a small hand-held torch, or briefly set ramekins beneath a very hot broiler until sugar is melted. Allow sugar to set, then chill in refrigerator for 10 minutes before serving.

Linden trees are common urban plantings because their dense foliage makes them great shade trees.

Making and using plant meal as a flour substitute

Technically, the definition of flour is "the finely ground meal of *grain*." But powdered meals suitable for use as flour substitutes can be made by drying and grinding many other edible plants. Flour mills are the perfect machine for this purpose, but they are very expensive. Thankfully, here is another means of making meal:

1. Thoroughly dry the plant material.
2. Place the dried plant material in a blender or food processor and turn the machine on high for a couple of minutes, until consistency is as close to flour as you can get it.
3. Using a sieve, separate coarse plant material from finer meal and discard coarse material.
4. Use flour right away or store in refrigerator or freezer for up to six months.

You can substitute up to a third of a recipe's flour with your plant meal, depending on what you're baking or cooking. Of the plants in this book, the following make excellent meals or flour substitutes:

Amaranth: Leaves, seeds

Cat's ear: Leaves

Clover: Flowers, leaves

Dandelion: Leaves

Dead nettle: Leaves, flowers

Dock: Leaves, seeds

Evening primrose: Leaves, roots, seeds

Lamb's-quarter: Leaves, seeds

Linden: Leaves (see recipe in this chapter)

Nettle: Leaves, seeds (seeds are a stimulant)

Nipplewort: Leaves

Plantain: Leaves, seeds

Wild carrot: Seeds (strong carrot flavor)

Wild fennel: Seeds, pollen

Bulrushes and native and invasive *Phragmites* (all in the Cyperaceae family) also make excellent flours. According to Linda Runyon's *The Essential Wild Food Survival Guide,* many common grasses found in the Gramineae family make good flours too:

Barley grass (*Hordeum pusillum nott*)

Barnyard grass (*Echinochloa crusgalli*)

Broomsedge (*Andropogon virginicus*)

Crabgrass (*Digitaria sanguinalis*)

Foxtail grass (*Setaria italica*)

Goosegrass (*Eleusine indica*)

Jungle grass (*Echinochloa colonum*)

Quackgrass (*Agropyron repens*)

Rye grass (*Lolium temulentum*)

Wild oats (*Avena fatua*)

Wild rice (*Zizania palustris*)

Yellow nutsedge (*Cyperus esculentus*)

Nipplewort

Common Nipplewort
Lapsana communis

Every time I utter the common name for this plant, people giggle: "You said 'nipple,' tee hee hee!" But if you can get past its name, nipplewort is one of the most versatile weeds to cook with, and it's very easy to find in the city. Because it has absolutely no bitter notes and is mildly flavored, I like to eat it raw in salads. But it's mild as a cooked green too and can be combined with many different foods without risk of competition between strong flavors.

Nipplewort is an herbaceous annual plant in the Asteraceae family. The genus name *Lapsana* comes from Lapsane, an edible herb described by the scholar Marcus Terentius Varro (116 BC–27 BC) of ancient Rome. The common name nipplewort is said to have been given by the famous English botanist John Parkinson (AD 1567–1650) after learning of its use in Prussia to heal chapped nipples. It had been used for this in Prussia and elsewhere in Europe due to the doctrine of signatures—both the closed flower buds and the lower leaf lobes were thought to resemble nipples.

Nipplewort is native to Europe and Southwest Asia and considered a pest weed in much of the United States. Nipplewort is the only species in its genus. The *Lapsana* genus originally contained five species, but in 1995 four of the species were moved to a different genus, leaving only *Lapsana communis* behind. (Of course, this makes absolutely no difference to the humble nipplewort—at least, there was no audible protest, so we continue to play our naming games).

Nipplewort was at one time cultivated as a vegetable, and there are still several common names in other languages that reflect this. Unfortunately, there is very little written about this plant. You'll just have to take my word and your own experimentation to know that it's a very worthwhile food plant.

IN THE FIELD

What It Looks Like: Typically 2–3 feet tall but can grow to 4 feet. Hairy stems and leaves. Leaves spirally arranged. Lower leaves up to 6 inches long and 2½ inches across. Each leaf typically has a large terminal lobe and two small side lobes. Terminal lobe and side lobes widely separated by very narrow segment of leaf blade, barely wider than the central vein. Terminal lobe usually broadly ovate with slight indentation at the base. Leaf edges toothed and slightly wavy or irregular. Lower leaves have long stems (petioles) slightly winged and hairy. Alternate upper leaves lack lobes, typically much narrower and lance shaped. Leaves become increasingly smaller as they ascend the stem. Flowers June to September. Central stem towers over side stems and terminates in loose cluster of composite flowers. Each composite flower ¼–½ inch across, consists of about 18–20 spreading ray florets (individual flowers that look like petals of the larger composite). Each ray floret pale yellow with a squared tip having five small teeth. Later in summer, ray florets replaced by curved, hairless seeds with several fine veins along their length. Spreads by reseeding. Seed sets July to October. Average plant has 1000 seeds; however, they don't remain viable as long as some other plant seeds do, and many do not germinate. Seed germinates in both autumn and spring. Seedlings that emerge in the autumn overwinter as small basal rosettes. Plants grow from a stout taproot.

Where to Find: Occurs throughout the United States

except Alabama, Delaware, Florida, Kansas, Louisiana, Mississippi, Nebraska, New Hampshire, Nevada, South Carolina, South Dakota, and Wyoming. Found in shady campgrounds, gravelly river bars, roadsides, alleys, wastelands, lawn edges. Grows in full sun to light shade, moist to dry conditions, loamy to gravelly soils.

When to Harvest: Young plants available as early as March. Leaves at best size and flavor in April and May. Leaves smaller and more tedious to collect in June and July.

What to Eat: Young leaves.

How to Harvest: Easily gathered by hand. Plant doesn't regenerate leaves after it's been picked, so it may be easier to pull up entire plant and finish processing it in your kitchen.

Poisonous Look-Alikes to Avoid: None.

IN THE KITCHEN

Why You Should Eat It: Nutritional value unknown or unavailable. It's in the same family as dandelion and cat's ear, so it probably shares some of the same nutritional value.

What It Tastes Like: Very little flavor. Slight bitterness sometimes detected in older plants.

How to Store: Wrap loosely in plastic bag in refrigerator for up to a week. Dry or blanch and freeze.

How to Cook: Use raw in salads or cooked like any other leafy green vegetable. Some people are put off by slight fuzziness of leaves. If so, dress salad before serving and/or chop leaves to a smaller size.

Nipplewort and Chickpea Coconut Curry

I like using a spicy curry blend for this recipe. Adding nipplewort not only tames the heat a bit, it introduces a clean vegetable flavor and texture to an otherwise thick, creamy dish. Because nipplewort is so mild, it does not interfere with the complexity of a good curry mix.

* SERVES 4 *

2 tablespoons ghee (clarified butter)
1 cup onion, coarsely chopped
2 tablespoons high quality curry powder
1 pound steamed nipplewort
1 cup stewed tomatoes with juice
8 ounces cooked chickpeas
½ cup coconut milk
2 pieces of na'an, halved

Place nipplewort in a steamer over simmering water. Cover and steam for 5 minutes.

Melt ghee in a large skillet over medium-high heat. Add onion and cook until softened. Stir in curry powder and cook 1 minute. Add nipplewort, tomatoes, chickpeas, and coconut milk. Season with additional curry if desired. Bring to a boil, reduce heat, and cover. Simmer 10 minutes. Serve with na'an.

Nipplewort, White Bean, and Sun-Dried Tomato Crostini

Along with bruschetta, crostini probably originated in medieval times when it was typical for Italian peasants to eat their meals on slices of bread rather than on dinnerware. I usually prepare something a little more substantial for the main course and serve this smaller dish as an appetizer.

* SERVES 4 *

1½ pounds nipplewort, chopped coarsely
1 tablespoon extra virgin olive oil
2 large garlic cloves, minced
2 cups cooked cannellini beans
    (19-ounce can, drained)
¼ cup sun-dried tomatoes packed in oil,
    finely chopped
½ teaspoon salt
freshly cracked pepper to taste
8 pieces of crostini

Place nipplewort in a steamer over simmering water. Cover and steam for 5 minutes.

Meanwhile, heat oil in a large skillet over medium heat. Add garlic and cook 30 seconds. Stir in beans, nipplewort, sun-dried tomatoes, salt, and pepper. Cook 2 minutes longer. Serve on crostini.

TOP Young nipplewort leaves usually, but don't always, have rounded tips, and many have small lobes near the stem. BOTTOM Most mature nipplewort leaves are lanceolate and have pointed tips, but some variety should be expected.

Stinging Nettle

Common Nettle, Great Stinging Nettle
Urtica dioica

Most everyone is familiar with stinging nettle, having stepped in it once or twice. I used to get "bit" just about every time I went backpacking. I learned of its edibility with the rest of my Brownie troop, so I've known for a long time. But every time I encountered a patch I lacked gloves, plus I was a little afraid that those little stingers might *not* disappear on cooking. Can you just imagine getting a mouthful of them? No thank you. So it took me years to get the nerve to finally collect, cook, and eat a plateful of them. I was finally seduced by the nutritional information and, once I tried them, well, there's just no going back. I really do love the flavor, so much so that I'm even willing to don gloves and boots on the hottest of days to harvest them. After learning of its exceptional value, and because I enjoy the flavor so much, I planted a garden of them in my front yard (see How to Grow Your Own Nettles sidebar).

Stinging nettle is an herbaceous perennial thought to be native to Europe, Asia, northern Africa, and North America. The word nettle may be from the Greek word for "irritated," *naton,* though some sources suggest the word is derived from *nodis,* Latin for "twisting or knotting," due to its value as a fiber plant. In Latin, *Urtica* means "burn." The word *dioica* is Latin for "two houses," a reference to nettles having male and female plants.

The top portions of the leaves are covered with tiny hairs that cause skin irritation. This stinging sensation comes from formic acid and histamine contained in the hollow hairs. Although stinging nettles can be a challenge to collect, nettle rash can be relieved by applying the juice of the leaves themselves, which takes away the stinging of the nettles.

People have been using stinging nettles for food, medicine, fiber, and dyes since the Bronze Age. Because of its many uses, Roma supposedly planted stinging nettle everywhere they went. Stinging nettles are one of the most valuable and delicious superfoods on the planet. They are common fare on European menus, and England even hosts an annual Stinging Nettle Eating Championship that draws thousands of people. They have just now begun showing up on US menus.

Medicinally, stinging nettles have been used to successfully treat myriad afflictions. They are still used to treat severe arthritis by exposing the patient's painful joints to direct contact with the plant. Although initially this is painful, arthritis sufferers insist stinging nettles numb their joint pain. As food, it is said to be very helpful as a boost for the immune system, especially for chronically ill people. This book does not thoroughly discuss medicinal uses, so I encourage you to research stinging nettles on your own.

Stinging nettles have many uses beyond just food and medicine. Their long, fibrous stems were used for weaving, cloth making, cordage, and even paper in parts of Europe. Native Americans used them for embroidery, fish nets, and other crafts. Unlike cotton, stinging nettles grow easily without pesticides. The tall stalks yield a stronger and finer fiber than flax. The Germans used this in place of cotton in World War II and have recently begun again producing commercial nettle textiles. A yellow dye can be extracted from the roots.

Stinging nettle is also valuable in the garden. Stinging nettle tea is given to houseplants to help them grow and sprayed on outdoor vegetation to control pests. Some say that if in the winter hens are given dry stinging nettles broken in small pieces with their food, they will fatten and increase egg production all winter long. When stinging nettle is cut and allowed to wilt, then used as fodder for livestock, it is known to increase milk production. In Egypt, oil from stinging nettle seeds is used in burning lamps. It's also a milk coagulant for pudding and cheese making.

IN THE FIELD

What It Looks Like: Grows to 7 feet tall in summer, dying down to the ground in winter. Widely spreading rhizomes and stolons. Soft green leaves 1–6 inches long are borne oppositely on erect, wiry, green stem. Leaves have strongly serrated edges, narrowly oval to heart-shaped. Small greenish flowers grow in tassel-like clusters from upper stem nodes. Blooms from July to September. Fruits small nutlets enclosed in dried sepals.

Where to Find: Occurs throughout the United States except Arkansas and Hawaii. Usually appears in same places year after year. Common in rich soil, disturbed habitats, moist woodlands, thickets, along rivers, along partially shaded trails. (Most any wooded trail you choose to hike wearing shorts.) Can be very abundant on wasteland, vacant lots, and pastures and in hedges.

When to Harvest: Leaves best collected in spring prior to flowering, but may be collected all season. Young leaves are best part of the plant, so many people collect only during spring. However, harvesting a portion of the plant encourages new growth, and if you limit yourself to upper third of each plant when you harvest, young leaves can be had well into fall. New plants typically come up in fall, and you can pick them before they're killed by frost.

What to Eat: Young stems and leaves. Flowers and seeds also edible, but may be stimulating like coffee.

How to Harvest: Collect them using work gloves, and wear a long-sleeved shirt. If you come upon a great nettle patch and no gloves are available, put your hand inside a plastic bag to pick. Some foragers insist that nettles can be picked bare-handed if you approach the task properly. Supposedly, if you come from underneath, then pull and grab the leaf, sort of like a folding a soft taco, you will not get stung. Unfortunately, this was not at all my experience

and I can't recommend it. If you get stung, rub dock, jewelweed, plantain, fern spores, or nettle juice onto the area for relief; you may have to do this every ten minutes for it to be effective.

Poisonous Look-Alikes to Avoid: None.

IN THE KITCHEN

Why You Should Eat It: High in calcium, magnesium, iron, potassium, phosphorus, and manganese. Excellent source of vitamins A and C, and high in B-complex vitamins. At its peak, stinging nettle contains up to 40 percent protein, dry weight—extraordinarily high for a leafy green vegetable. Stinging nettle seeds are thought to support adrenal function; the chronically tired take them as a caffeine-free stimulant.

Who Should Avoid It: After stinging nettle enters its flowering and seed setting stages, lower, older leaves develop gritty particles called cystoliths, which can irritate the urinary tract.

What It Tastes Like: Some sources say that raw stinging nettles taste like green beans. Their cooked flavor is very similar to spinach.

How to Store: Steam and freeze or dry. Fresh leaves keep in refrigerator between moist paper towels for a day or two, but expect some wilt.

How to Cook: Wear rubber gloves to clean and chop stinging nettles. Alternatively, *thoroughly* soak stinging nettles in water for 20 minutes or briefly steam them to remove the stinging chemicals so they can be further handled and safely eaten. Juicing and blending also remove the source of stinging. For nearly raw salad greens, place leaves in hot water for a few seconds, then plunge into cold water. Thorough drying also removes the stinging chemicals.

Cream of Stinging Nettle Soup

This recipe is a longtime classic among foragers, but I chose to include it in this book anyway because it is delicious and perhaps the best way to showcase the wonderful flavor of stinging nettles. It should come as no surprise that my version contains about twice the garlic of most other recipes.

* SERVES 6 *

4 tablespoons butter
2 shallots, chopped
1 teaspoon salt
1 pound potatoes, peeled and cubed
2 cups vegetable or chicken broth
½ pound stinging nettle leaves
2 large cloves garlic, minced
½ teaspoon white pepper
½ teaspoon ground pepper
¼ teaspoon Chinese five spice
2 cups milk
½ cup sour cream or yogurt

Melt butter in a large pot. Add shallots and salt; cook until shallots are soft. Add potatoes and broth and bring to a boil. Reduce heat and simmer for 15 minutes. Add nettles and garlic and cook until very tender, about 10 minutes. Add pepper, five spice, and additional salt to taste.

Puree soup with an immersion blender or in a food processor (in batches if necessary). For the smoothest texture, soup may be poured through a sieve. Pour puree back into large pot. Add milk and mix thoroughly. Warm to serving temperature over medium-low heat. Serve with a dollop of sour cream or yogurt.

Stinging Nettle and Goat Cheese Crêpes

Crepes make just about anything seem fancy, even cooked weeds. I like serving them as "spinach and cheese crêpes," then only after guests exclaim how wonderful they are do I let them in on my little secret: they have just eaten stinging nettles.

* SERVES 4 *

CRÊPES
1 cup flour
2 eggs
½ cup milk
½ cup water
¼ teaspoon salt
2 tablespoons butter, melted

FILLING
¼ onion, chopped
2 tablespoons olive oil
1 clove garlic, minced
2 cups loosely packed fresh nettle leaves
½ teaspoon sea salt or to taste
¼ cup white wine
4 ounces chèvre (goat cheese)
1 tablespoon minced fresh thyme
½ cup sour cream

To make the crêpes, in a large mixing bowl whisk together flour and eggs. Gradually add milk and water, stirring to combine. Add salt and butter. Beat until smooth.

Heat a lightly oiled griddle or frying pan over medium-high heat. Pour or scoop ¼ cup batter onto the griddle for each crêpe. Tilt pan with a circular motion so batter coats surface evenly. When surface of crêpe is dry, remove from pan and place on a plate. Continue making crêpes until batter is gone, separating each crêpe with a sheet of wax paper.

To make the filling, sauté onion in olive oil over medium heat until softened. Stir in garlic, nettles and salt. Immediately add white wine. Cook another minute, or until wine is nearly all cooked off.

To assemble, place a crêpe, browned side down, on a serving platter. Place 2 tablespoons of nettle mixture near one end of crêpe. Place a heaping tablespoon (about an ounce) chèvre (goat cheese) on top of the nettles. Starting with the filling side, loosely roll up the crêpe. Garnish with sour cream and fresh thyme. Repeat until filling is gone.

Note: If you have leftover crêpes, place them in a resealable plastic bag, leaving wax paper intact, and freeze for up to six months. Thaw and briefly heat when you're ready to use them.

> Tender handed stroke
> a nettle
> And it will sting you for your pains.
> But grasp it like a man
> of mettle
> And it soft as silk remains.
>
> —Traditional English saying

How to grow your own nettles

To grow nettles from seed, collect seeds in the fall. In the spring, plant them indoors. Barely cover the seeds with soil; they should germinate within two weeks. Once the seedlings are a few inches tall, transplant them to full sun or partial shade, spacing them about a foot apart. Nettles can grow to 5 feet or more, so don't plant them under a tree with low branches. They are perennial down to –30°F and can grow in warm climates as well. Also be aware that nettles spread by running roots, so give them plenty of space and don't plant them next to your favorite patch of flowers.

You can also start nettles by harvesting and planting a piece of root. To grow nettles indoors, place the rhizomes in a pot filled with earth and keep it inside for the winter. The plants are not likely to grow very tall, but the young shoots are a nice treat when greens can't be found outdoors.

You can even transplant a whole plant to your garden outdoors; the plant may die back for the rest of the season, but it should resume its growth the following spring.

Stinging nettle leaves are very obviously serrated and
grow in alternating opposite pairs.

Wild Carrot

Queen Anne's Lace, Bird's Nest Weed,
Devils Plague, Bird's Nest Root, Fools Parsley, Lace Flower
Daucus carota

When I was a kid, my maternal grandparents were dairy farmers in northern Wisconsin. I would visit every couple years during the summer and walk the pastures with my grandma to help guide the milk cows into the barn every evening. Back then, the fields were closely grazed, almost like a park or a golf course were it not for the cow patties.

Their farm eventually went under, as did many small farms in the Midwest. Wild carrot was one of the first colonizers of my grandma's "born-again" prairie. In the ensuing summers, instead of herding the cows in, we'd walk the field to collect bouquets of goldenrod, purple aster, and this lovely white lace. We had no knowledge then about how tasty the leaves, flowers, and roots of this plant are.

Wild carrot is the wild progenitor of the garden carrots we are familiar with today and, in fact, shares the same botanical name. It's an herbaceous biennial and, along with parsley, anise, caraway, celery, and dill, belongs to the Umbelliferae (also known as the Apiaceae) family. All members of this family bear their flowers and fruits in umbels. The word umbel is from the Latin word for parasol, *umbell,* and indeed the flowers are reminiscent of opened umbrellas. The genus name *Daucus* comes from *daukos,* a name the Greeks gave to several members of the Umbelliferae family. *Daukos* may be derived from *daîo,* Greek for "overheated one." The species name *carota* means "carrot" in Latin. The common name wild carrot was given by William Turner in 1548.

There are several stories behind the common name Queen Anne's lace. One of the more well-known claims that Queen Anne of Great Britain (1664–1714), a talented lace maker, challenged her ladies-in-waiting to create a lace as beautiful as the flowers in her garden. Queen Anne herself won the contest and named her dear flower after herself. The legend goes that the deep red floret in the plant's center was a drop of blood spilled from the queen's finger as she made the lace. Others have suggested the name of the plant comes from Saint Anne, the mother of the Virgin Mary and the patron saint of lace makers.

Wild carrot is native to Eurasia and North Africa and is thought to have initially spread via the Silk Road and later by European colonization. A rather cosmopolitan traveler, it can now readily be found in much of the rest of the world. Botanists claim that worldwide, there are more than 12 varieties of the wild carrot species. In North America, we have two varieties, an annual and a biennial.

As you might guess, wild carrot features a long taproot, though it is not nearly as large in diameter as that of our domestic carrots. If you dig one up, however, and do the scratch and sniff test, you will find that it smells just like a garden carrot, perhaps slightly stronger. Though the roots are edible when young, their centers become tough and woody. Domestic carrots have been hybridized to eliminate much of this woodiness.

The beautiful compound flowers of wild carrot form soft parasols of hundreds of tiny white florets. Often, in the center of the inflorescence, there is a single dark red floret standing tall above the sea of white. Botanists have long debated the possible reasons for its development. Many earlier botanists believed it was a genetic mutation that was of no particular service to the plant. But today's botanists disagree, suggesting the colored floret may trick potential pollinators such as predatory wasps into thinking there is food on the flower. Still others believe the presence of an apparent "insect" may be a signal to other insects that the plant is a source of nectar, thereby attracting other pollinators. Scientists hope that solving the question of the dark spot's function may lead to future agricultural developments and methods for improving cultivated carrots.

Wild carrot was in use long before it was ever hybridized to the carrot we know today. Sometime between 500 and 400 BC, Hippocrates wrote about its medicinal uses. Ancient folklore claims one should eat the dark colored spot in the middle of the flower to cure epilepsy.

Even now, herbalists use wild carrot to treat a wide variety of ailments. Many still use the seeds to counter flatulence and colic. Several promising studies underway are beginning to show wild carrot may be useful in many areas of alternative medicine, for example as a treatment for Alzheimer's, Crohn's disease, Parkinson's disease, infertility, certain types of cancer, diabetes, and leukemia. And recent studies are proving out the efficacy of its longtime usage as a "morning after" contraceptive tea.

Beyond medicine, an essential oil obtained from the seed is used cosmetically in anti-wrinkle creams. Also, a strong decoction of the seeds and root are said to make

As the wild carrot flower blooms it resembles a cup-like basket.

a very good insecticide. In North America, wild carrot is considered a noxious weed in several states. Weed or not, it makes a beautiful cut flower and is therefore quite popular among commercial florists.

IN THE FIELD

What It Looks Like: Grows 2–4 feet tall. Stems erect, hairy, hollow, vertically grooved, branched at top. Leaves basal, alternate, pinnately compound with finely divided, fernlike leaflets. During first year, leaves emerge as a basal rosette; rosette remains green over winter. During second year, a stem emerges and the plant flowers and sets seed. Emergence of flower stem is called bolting. Upper leaves of second-year plants stalkless with white sheaths at leaf bases. Small white flowers with five petals borne in umbel at ends of stems. Plants may have secondary umbels at any node on the stem, will produce a succession of flowering stalks until they die back with the first frost. As umbels produce achenes (seedlike fruits containing seeds), umbel closes upward into a cup or bird's nest shape. Small, dry, brown achenes ribbed with bristly hairs, have hooked spines that attach to clothing or animal fur. One plant can produce 1000–40,000 seeds. Most seeds germinate within two years of dispersal, but may persist in soil for up to seven years. Plants generally fertilized by a large variety of insect species; however, self-fertilization may also occur. Root a long, slender, white to pale yellow taproot with fibrous secondary roots. Roots become woody with age. Characteristic odor of carrot detectable when any part of plant bruised or severed.

Where to Find: Occurs throughout the United States. Prefers well-drained, alkaline or neutral, sandy, gravelly soils in full or partial sun. Commonly seen in disturbed grasslands, fields, meadows, pastures, ditches, waste places, and railroad and highway rights-of-way

When to Harvest: Gather flowers from late June through August. Harvest entire plant in July and dry for later use. Collect first-year roots in spring. Gather shoots from spring into fall, as first-year plants may emerge as early as March and continue to emerge until mid-October. Gather seeds in fall.

What to Eat: Young taproots, flowers, shoots, leaves, seeds.

How to Harvest: Use a shovel to harvest wild carrot roots, but be warned they may be difficult to remove when growing in tightly packed sand and gravel. Cut flowers well above the node to allow plant to produce a new bolt from below the cut. Collect seeds by shaking them loose in a paper bag.

Poisonous Look-Alikes to Avoid: Extreme caution must be used when collecting wild carrots, as they closely resemble poison hemlock (*Conium maculatum*), which can be deadly. Fortunately, there are a few simple ways to tell the difference. Poison hemlock has a rather offensive odor, while wild carrot, especially the root, smells like carrots. Also, the wild carrot stem is hairy, whereas the poison hemlock stem is smooth. Poison hemlock has smooth hollow stalks with purple splotches. See chapter 6, Poisonous Weeds Common to Urban Areas, for more information.

IN THE KITCHEN

Why You Should Eat It: Contains respectable levels of pectin, a substance thought to lower cholesterol. Good source of vitamin A, potassium, thiamin, niacin, vitamin B6, folate, manganese, and fiber.

Who Should Avoid It: Root of wild carrot can induce uterine contractions and so should not be used by pregnant women. Leaves contain furocoumarins, which may cause allergic contact dermatitis for some people, with later exposure to the sun resulting in mild photodermatitis.

What It Tastes Like: A strong version of a garden carrot. Roots more fibrous than domesticated carrots.

How to Store: Cook and freeze or can the root. Dry any part of or the entire plant for later use as a flavoring.

How to Cook: Bake or boil roots. Deep-fry umbels and/or leaves for fritters. Use any part of the plant raw and finely chopped as a salad addition.

Wild Carrot Flower Tempura

I can't think of a more beautiful flower to cook as a tempura dish. With its distinctly carroty flavor, this dish makes a very appealing appetizer or garnish with servings of meat or fish. To eat this delicacy, hold a cooked flower by its stem and place part or all of the umbel in your mouth. Loosely close your teeth around the main stem and slowly pull it away from your mouth. The bracts and coarser stems will be drawn out of your mouth so you eat only the tender flowers.

❋ MAKES 20 ❋

1 egg
1 cup flour
1 tablespoon cornstarch
½ teaspoon salt
1 cup olive oil
1½ cups seltzer water, ice cold
20 freshly cut flower heads, at least 6 inches
   of stem intact
Kosher salt to taste

Whisk egg, flour, cornstarch, and salt together. Set aside.

In a medium skillet, heat oil over medium-high heat. When oil is hot, whisk cold seltzer water into flour mixture, then immediately dip the flowers in this batter.

Wearing an oven mitt, use tongs to grasp each flower by its stem and submerge the flower head in hot oil. Hold the flower, face side down, in the oil until golden brown, about 15 seconds. Remove and place on a paper towel, stem up. Sprinkle with kosher salt. Repeat this process for remaining flowers.

Note: You can also use a deep fryer to cook several flowers at a time, but the one-at-a-time approach makes for a better presentation.

Wild Carrot Soufflé

This dish delights the senses on so many levels. Its towering yellow fluff holds visual appeal, though it doesn't rise quite as much as a traditional soufflé; the smell of cooked carrot is mouthwatering; the creamy texture is comforting—and the combination of flavors is exquisite.

* SERVES 4 *

½ pound wild carrot roots, peeled and
   chopped
½ cup sugar
¾ teaspoon baking powder
1 teaspoon vanilla
1 tablespoon all-purpose flour
2 eggs, beaten
¼ cup unsalted butter, softened
1 teaspoon powdered sugar

Preheat oven to 350°F. In a large pot of boiling water, cook carrots until very tender. Drain and transfer to a large mixing bowl. Add sugar, baking powder, and vanilla, and beat in until smooth. Mix in flour, eggs, and butter. Spoon resulting batter into four 13½-ounce buttered porcelain soufflé dishes or ramekins. Bake 30 minutes or until tops are golden brown. Sprinkle lightly with powdered sugar and serve immediately.

Wild carrot stems are obviously hairy while poisonous look-alikes have smooth stems; the leaves look very similar to garden-carrot leaves.

The urban-wild salad

There's no better way to celebrate the first signs of spring than making a salad of wild (okay, urban) mixed greens. Our word "salad" comes from the Latin *salata*, or "salted herbs," and throughout much of our history, raw leafy greens were indeed eaten with oil, vinegar, and/or salt.

The difference between yesterday's salad and today's? Our leafy green selection has shrunk to just a few kinds of lettuce and spinach. Variety is the spice of life not only because it tastes better, but because it's better for our health. So which weeds lend themselves to salad fixings? Here are 20 of my favorite leafy greens for the wild urban salad:

Amaranth: treat leaves like spinach

Chickweed: top third, before plant flowers if possible

Clover: flowers only (use leaves for cooking), chop coarsely or leave whole

Creeping wood sorrel: remove stems

Dandelion: leaves, midrib removed; flowers, green bracts and stems removed, best before going to seed

Daylily: shoots and flower buds, chopped or left intact

Evening primrose: shoots, young leaves, flowers, flower buds

Hairy bittercress: leaves from early basal rosette

Honesty: flowers, young leaves, young silicles (seedpods)

Lamb's-Quarter: treat leaves like spinach

Linden: leaves, blossoms

Mallow: leaves, flowers

Nipplewort: leaves, chopped to ½ inch

Purslane: chopped or whole

Sheep sorrel: leaves, chopped or whole

Sow thistle: leaves, chopped, best before flowering

Wild carrot: leaves and flowers, chopped and not more than 5 percent of total salad greens

Wild fennel: fronds, flowers, immature seeds

Wild mustard: not more than 20 percent of the total salad greens

Wild pea: shoots, chopped or whole

I like dressing such a salad with a simple vinaigrette so the complex flavors aren't lost and because vinegar helps your body absorb more of the salad's nutrition:

VINAIGRETTE

1 tablespoon cider or balsamic vinegar

3 tablespoons extra virgin olive oil

¼ teaspoon salt

¼ teaspoon pepper

Mix all ingredients together and dress your urban-wild salad with it.

Horta vrasta (Boiled leafy greens)

The "Mediterranean Diet" has been on the dieticians' radar for at least 20 years now. Pasta, olives, olive oil, red wine, cheese, and pizza are some of the foods that come to mind when you think of the Mediterranean. Boiled greens—not so much.

Imagine a place where a bowl of cooked leafy greens is so well loved that they actually have a name for it! There is such a place: Greece. Boiled greens, or *horta vrasta* (HOR-tah vrah-STAH), is a Greek staple.

On the Greek island of Crete, the hillsides are lush with wild leafy greens (weeds), many of which the Cretans are known to pick and eat almost daily. The greens are boiled and served with a generous amount of olive oil and fresh lemon; lemon helps the body absorb vegetable-based calcium. When sweeter greens are used, the dish is called *horta vrasta, vlita, antidia,* or *zochi*. When bitter greens are used, it's known as *radikia* or *xorta tou vounou*.

Delicious and easy to prepare, *horta vrasta* packs a huge nutritional punch with each spoonful—think Popeye's can of spinach times ten. I have a hunch that these greens have more to do with the Cretans' 80-plus average life expectancy than the wine and cheese do.

You can use *any* of the greens discussed in this book to make *horta vrasta*. Boiled greens wilt down when cooked, so be sure to pick five or six times the volume of greens as the volume you hope to serve as a finished dish. Four servings generally require a good three pounds of fresh greens.

Simply bring a large pot of water to a boil, submerge the greens, and cook for about 20 minutes or until the thickest parts of the stems are tender. Don't overdo it, or you will lose all the nutritional goodness into the cooking water (although you can always drink the chilled cooking water later as an afternoon health tonic). Drain the greens in a colander, then place them in a serving bowl and dress with extra virgin olive oil, lemon juice, salt, and pepper. Serve the greens warm or at room temperature.

Though it's not the traditional Greek style, you might consider steaming the greens rather than boiling them to retain more of their vitamins and minerals.

5 | VACANT LOTS AND ROADSIDES

I tend to think of the weeds in this chapter as the "homeless" among the plant world. Most of them don't grow well in pampered, stiffly maintained areas. However, they are strong-willed enough to thrive in the face of the cruelest neglect. Most of these plants are drought tolerant, fertilizer averse, and actually prefer areas like vacant lots and gravel shoulders over cushier spots like parks, gardens, and lawns.

As discussed in chapter 1, take precautions against vehicle traffic, feral dogs, used needles, broken glass, and contamination related to heavy traffic or past commercial or industrial land use. Whenever practical, make an attempt, at least, to contact the owner of a vacant lot.

The above cautions may cause you to think that vacant lots and roadsides aren't worth the trouble. But some of the most healthful and best-tasting weeds grow in such locations. They are indeed well worth the effort. And note, you can find them growing in many other urban spaces too.

Dock

Sorrel, Bitter Dock, Broad-Leaved Dock
Rumex obtusifolius

In late summer and through fall, dock plants bear reddish-brown sprays of dried seeds. As kids, my brothers and I referred to it as Indian tobacco. I'm not sure where we got this idea. Maybe because we thought it looked similar to the Prince Albert tobacco my dad loaded his pipe with. Or because we watched a fair number of old westerns and wanted something with which to fill our toy peace pipes (the ones decorated with feathers dyed in colors rarely found in nature).

For me, its appeal actually lay mostly in the satisfaction of sliding my hand up the stem to gather a giant fistful of seeds. After crunching them up in my fist a bit, further sampling whatever sensation could be had from a handful of seeds, I'd do my best imitation of Old MacDonald and scatter them to the soil. Because my scattering activity generally occurred in my mother's vegetable garden, dock was likely one of the weeds she fought most tenaciously. It's too bad she did not know that her garden enemy could be enticed into friendship using nothing more than a soup pot.

Dock is a large, herbaceous perennial plant with a deep taproot reaching up to 5 feet deep. It was brought from Europe to North America by early settlers as a food plant. The genus name *Rumex* comes from the Latin word *rumo*, which was taken from the Greek word *rufo*, meaning "to suck," possibly because there are accounts of early Romans using it to stave off thirst. The species name *obtusifolius* generally refers to a leaf with a rounded tip. The common name dock refers to undesirable weeds that were cut and removed, or docked (like docking an animal's tail).

Dock is one of the early colonizers of bare ground, and it's commonly found where soil has recently been disturbed. When cooked, dock loses its green color, but don't let that put you off. As noted 17th-century botanist Nicholas Culpeper once scolded, "Women will not put dock into a pot, because it makes the pottage black; pride and ignorance (a couple of monsters in the creation) preferring nicety before health." I would argue that dock does not turn black, more of a tan to gray color. I used to think of dock as a pest weed, but that was before I tried the young leaves in a salad. Because they contain oxalic acid, they are pleasantly tart, almost lemony.

Dock has long been used in herbal medicine. Besides being used as medicine and eaten as a potherb, dock leaves were used to wrap farmhouse butter.

Dock is the bane of many a farmer, as it can be toxic to some livestock and it's a common agricultural weed. Seeds can lie dormant for many years, and eradication is challenging. In addition, the taproots of established plants have a large reserve of energy, allowing plants to tolerate repeated defoliation (a plus for the edible-weed enthusiast).

IN THE FIELD

What It Looks Like: Very large leaves, some lower ones with red stems. Edges of leaves slightly wavy. Foliage can grow to about 18 inches in height. Bases of stems covered by thin, papery sheath, a key characteristic of the buckwheat family. Leaves in a basal rosette. As young leaves emerge from center of plant, they appear as tightly rolled cylinders typically wet with mucilage they exude at base of plant. Cylinders unfurl about a week after they first emerge, growing sometimes as large as 2 feet long and 1 foot wide. Small green flowers born in large clusters on a single stalk above leaves bloom from June through September.

Reddish-brown seeds, produced in late summer and fall, have toothed wing structures, allowing them to be dispersed by wind or water and also to attach to animals or machinery to be spread great distances. This description also applies to curly dock, *Rumex crispus*, except that its leaves are narrower and have wavier margins.

Where to Find: Throughout North America, including continental United States as well as Alaska and Hawaii. Commonly found in urban areas in vacant lots, rubble dumps, urban meadows, highway banks, drainage ditches, along railroad tracks, in neglected ornamental landscapes. Thrives in nutrient-rich, damp soil but can grow well in a variety of soil conditions.

When to Harvest: Young stalks and leaves in spring, larger leaves through summer, seeds in fall through winter.

What to Eat: Leaves, shoots, stems, and seeds.

How to Harvest: Collect leaves by hand in spring or use scissors or snips if necessary in summer. Gather seeds by handfuls in fall.

Poisonous Look-Alikes to Avoid: None.

IN THE KITCHEN

Why You Should Eat It: High in calcium, potassium, and vitamin C. Pound for pound, dock contains more vitamin A than carrots. Also a good source of vitamins B1, B2, and iron. Oxalic acid lends a tart taste; dock can be used in recipes that call for rhubarb. Seeds are high in protein.

Who Should Avoid It: Due to its oxalic acid content, it is not recommended for people with kidney problems. See Oxalic Acid sidebar in chapter 3.

What It Tastes Like: Leaf flavor is lemony, tart, citrus-like. Cooked, leaves taste like other mildly flavored cooked greens such as spinach. Seeds have a slightly nutty flavor.

How to Store: Place in a vase or glass of water on kitchen counter or between damp paper towels in refrigerator crisper. Dry as an herb. Store dried seeds in a sealed container in a dark place.

How to Cook: Eat shoots and young leaves raw in salads. Older leaves become tough and should be cooked. Historically, some cooked the leaves in milk to reduce astringency due to tannins. Depending on texture you're after, you

can either leave the midribs intact or remove them. Use the midribs themselves, as well as the peeled young blossom stalks, as an asparagus substitute; some people pickle them. Grind the seeds (husks and all) into a powder to add to hot cereal or to flour to make bread.

Dock Pesto

Pesto's popularity didn't really get a foothold in the United States until the late 1980s. Perhaps someone tried to serve it using the English translation, "paste," and it just didn't take off. One day someone may have had the brilliant notion to keep the Italian name pesto, *and people were willing to try it. One thing is for sure: one bite, and you will be sold. Most pestos, including this one, include grated hard cheese, ground nuts, olive oil, garlic, and some type of leafy greens. Making pesto with raw dock is a great way to preserve its lovely shade of green.*

* MAKES ABOUT 1 ½ CUPS *

2 cups packed, coarsely chopped dock leaves
3 large cloves garlic
¼ cup hazelnuts
⅔ cup extra virgin olive oil
½ cup grated Romano cheese
½ teaspoon each sea salt and fresh ground
    pepper or to taste

Combine dock, garlic, and hazelnuts in a food processor. Pulse until chopped. Add ½ cup oil and process until smooth. Add cheese, salt, and pepper. Pulse just until blended. Add remaining oil and pulse two or three more times. Taste and adjust seasoning. Serve immediately or transfer to an air-tight container and freeze (dock pesto can be stored frozen for up to one year).

Six delicious ways to use your wild greens pesto

You can substitute any wild green, cup for cup, for dock in making pesto. Here are some ways to put your wild-greens pestos to use.

1. **Pesto on rustic artisanal bread.** Looking for a very quick potluck offering or dinner party fin ger food? Buy or bake your favorite rustic bread and cut it into 2-inch cubes. Serve it with pesto in two separate bowls. Now watch it disappear.
2. **Pesto with pasta.** Thaw a cup of pesto or make it fresh. Add to hot, drained pasta and blend well. If you have time to dress it up, add fresh chopped tomatoes and garnish with a couple of large shavings of Romano or Pecorino cheese.
3. **Pesto pizza.** Substitute pesto for pizza sauce on prepared pizza crusts or homemade pizza. Additional toppings optional.
4. **Potatoes and pesto.** Change it up! Butter and sour cream are so yesterday.
5. **Fish and pesto.** Spread pesto inside the fish's body cavity or over a fillet. This is especially good with wild salmon.
6. **Pesto and farm-fresh eggs.** Yes. Eggs. Trust me, it's delicious.

Dock Shoots Szechwan-Style

Dock's lemony flavor goes perfectly with garlic and ginger. Add a little crushed red pepper to this Asian fusion dish, and you will think you're in south-central China. Don't worry about the shoots' gelatinous coating. Most of it disappears when cooked, and what remains actually gives the dish a nice mouth feel.

* SERVES 4 *

DOCKSHOOTS
- 20 young dock shoots, 5–8 inches in length
- ¼ cup olive oil
- 3 large cloves garlic, minced
- 1 tablespoon grated fresh ginger
- 1 to 2 teaspoons crushed red pepper
- ½ teaspoon salt or to taste
- 2 scallions, coarsely chopped, for garnish

DIPPING SAUCE
- 1 tablespoon sugar
- ½ cup warm water
- 3 tablespoons canola oil
- 1 clove garlic, minced
- 1 teaspoon grated fresh ginger
- 1 teaspoon soy sauce
- 1 tablespoon rice vinegar

To prepare the dock, preheat broiler. In a shallow pan, roll dock shoots in olive oil until coated. Sprinkle 3 cloves minced garlic, 1 tablespoon grated ginger, red pepper, and salt over the dock. Broil for 1–2 minutes, stirring once or twice.

To make the dipping sauce, dissolve sugar in warm water. Add oil, 1 clove minced garlic, 1 teaspoon grated ginger, soy sauce, and rice vinegar; whisk until combined.

Serve dock warm, alone or over a small portion of brown rice. Garnish with chopped scallions. Serve dipping sauce in a small bowl.

Weed Seed Crackers

The seeds of many edible weeds make excellent ingredients for homemade seed crackers.

∗ MAKES 20-30 CRACKERS ∗

1 cup dock seed meal (see Making and Using Plant Meal as a Flour Substitute sidebar in chapter 4)
1 cup whole wheat or other flour of your choice
½ cup grated Parmesan or other hard cheese
2 tablespoons primrose seeds
2 tablespoons lamb's-quarter seeds
2 tablespoons plantain seeds
1 tablespoons wild fennel or wild carrot seeds
1 teaspoon salt
water
vegetable oil spray (coconut or olive work great)

Preheat oven to 375°F. Mix flours, cheese, seeds, and salt. Using your hands to knead, add enough water to make a pliable but not too sticky dough. Between two pieces of parchment paper, roll the dough as thinly as you can.

Spray oil on baking sheet. Cut dough into desired shapes and place on baking sheet. Alternatively, transfer the dough whole and break apart after baking. Bake for 10–12 minutes or until crisp.

OPPOSITE Dock seed heads, with their rusty red color, are a familiar sight in late summer.

Evening Primrose

Common Evening Primrose, Sundrops, Suncups
Oenothera biennis

We often have vivid memories of when we were first introduced to a plant, and I have just such a memory with my introduction to evening primrose. The most fun summer camp I ever attended was with the Youth Conservation Corps, a federally funded organization that once employed low-income teens in environmental preservation jobs throughout the nation. Typically, teens worked on several different tasks during their stay, ranging from cleaning outhouses to building hiking trails. My favorite job was cutting birch and alder saplings from a young pine forest. It was my favorite because I liked working with the hacksaw and it took place in a recently logged area lush with evening primrose, pearly everlasting, and fireweed. I'll never forget learning the names of those plants from my camp counselor who, like me, had an affinity for wildflowers. Back then, I didn't know evening primrose could be eaten. I've always had a special fondness for these soft yellow flowers, but even more now that I know how useful they are in the kitchen.

Evening primrose is an herbaceous perennial native to North America. *Oenothera* is Latin for "a plant whose juices may cause sleep," and indeed it has been used for many centuries for its sedative qualities. Another of evening primrose's common names is king's cure-all because it's credited with healing numerous maladies including headaches, baldness, and laziness.

Just before nightfall, its flowers open quite suddenly to release a subtle but deliciously sweet perfume. It takes each flower only about a minute to go from closed bud to fully open, and flowers remain open until midmorning the following day. Pollination is mostly by moths, but also by some species of bees. As the plant matures, flowers also bloom in the daytime. It's noted for attracting wildlife, and the seeds are a good food source for birds.

Evening primrose was once cultivated for its edible roots but fell out of favor with introduction of the potato. Some Native American tribes rubbed the root on athletes to give them strength and good luck in hunting. The primrose was and still is to some extent used to treat a wide variety of ailments including rheumatism, paralysis, gout, wounds, headaches, insomnia, chest problems, and mood disorders. Today it is commercially grown for its medicinal oil and is widely used to treat premenstrual syndrome (PMS) and as an omega-3-6-9 fatty acid supplement.

Due to their ability to tolerate drought conditions, a number of evening primrose species are commonly used in landscapes, particularly in the arid Southwest. Plants self-sow freely and easily naturalize in the wild garden.

IN THE FIELD

What It Looks Like: Grows to 4–5 feet tall. Smooth, lanceolate leaves grow in a basal rosette at ground level, then spiral up to flowering stems. Stems of second-year plants erect, stout, hairy, reddish, branching to form a shrub. Leaves hairy, lanceolate, about 3–6 inches long, alternate. Flower spikes about 2½ inches in diameter grow along stalk on auxiliary branches. Flowers have four pale to bright yellow petals, and a cross-shaped stigma. Fruit an oblong capsule, about 1 inch long, containing numerous tiny reddish seeds. Long, fibrous taproot yellow on outside with lighter, nearly white interior. Frost-hardy.

Where to Find: Occurs throughout the United States, except Arizona, Colorado, Hawaii, Idaho, Utah, and

Wyoming. Acts as a primary colonizer, quickly appearing in patches of bare earth. Often found in poor, dry soils such as roadsides, railway embankments, and wastelands. Also found in meadows and cultivated beds. Prefers sandy or loamy, well-drained soils; does not tolerate shade well.

When to Harvest: Younger leaves in early summer. Collect flowers June through September. Seeds ripen from August to October. Select tender first-year roots.

What to Eat: Entire plant, including seedpods.

How to Harvest: Search ground near a stand of second-year plants to find roots of first-year plants. First-year rosettes easily identified by their lanceolate leaves with distinctive white midribs. Leaves, flowers, and seeds can be gathered like any other weed's.

Poisonous Look-Alikes to Avoid: None.

Young evening primrose seed heads have a peppery flavor and can be sautéed or steamed.

Why You Should Eat It: Rich in omega-3 fatty acids as well as gamma-linolenic acid, a rare form of omega-6 not found in many plant sources that has numerous vital functions in the body. Today the seed oil is used as a dietary supplement, to reduce PMS pain, and to treat mood disorders.

Who Should Avoid It: Some side effects of using concentrated evening primrose *oil* are itching, sore throat, and severe or extreme gassiness. Lowers the threshold for epileptic seizures, so it should be avoided in those cases; also, combining evening primrose *oil* with phenothiazines can trigger seizures. Caution advised for those on anticoagulants. Evening primrose *oil* may cause headaches and nausea on an empty stomach and diarrhea with high doses. All of these concerns are limited to the use of the concentrated oil, not the entire plant.

What It Tastes Like: Roots have a peppery taste often compared to parsnips and can be sweet and succulent. Flowers are sweet with a mild lemon pepper bite. Leaves also taste mildly peppery with a hint of lemon.

How to Store: Keep dried seeds in airtight containers. Store leaves in a loosely closed plastic bag in refrigerator up to two days. Store roots in a cool, dark location for a month or more. Use flowers right away.

How to Cook: Eat young roots like a vegetable boiled or baked. Eat shoots raw in salads. Steam or sauté young seedpods. Use dried seeds in place of sesame or poppy seeds; to take full advantage of the health benefits of the seeds' oils, crush them prior to adding them to a recipe. Flowers best eaten raw. Use leaves in salads, soups, and stews like any other leafy green; however, they are quite pungent and somewhat hairy, so they're best chopped small and mixed with other greens when eaten raw.

Evening Primrose Root Roast

This makes a satisfying fall dish when many perennial roots (as well as humans like me) are plumping up with starch in preparation for the cold season. Evening primrose roots are peppery when raw, but cooking tames the flavor to something between radish and parsnip. The seeds, which retain their peppery flavor through cooking, are used as a spice in this recipe.

* SERVES 4 *

20 mature evening primrose seedpods
3 tablespoons olive oil
½ pound evening primrose roots, peeled
   and sliced in half lengthwise
¼ pound wild carrots or ½ pound
   garden carrots, peeled and sliced
   in half lengthwise
3 tablespoons honey
1 tablespoon soy sauce
⅛ cup orange juice
zest of 1 orange

Preheat oven to 400°F. Remove seeds from pods, place on a baking pan, and roast for 10 minutes. Remove from oven and set aside.

Pour oil into a roasting pan and put into oven to heat. Add primrose roots and carrots and toss to coat. Season to taste with salt and pepper. Roast for 20 minutes.

Mix honey, soy, juice, and zest. Add to roots and toss to coat. Return to oven for another 10 minutes until caramelized. Season with roasted seeds and serve immediately.

Evening Primrose Salad

Evening primrose continues to blossom well after its first seedpods develop, thus you can collect the flowers and seedpods simultaneously. This is good because they go together very nicely in a summer salad. It's a rare treat to eat a dish comprised of nearly every part of a single plant. (Heck, if you have any evening primrose roots or seeds, you could throw them in too!) But though the novelty is certainly fun, the flavors are what make it worthy of the dining room table.

* SERVES 2 *

½ cup young evening primrose seedpods
2 tablespoons primrose or extra virgin
   olive oil
1 tablespoon apple cider vinegar
1 teaspoon minced fresh thyme
Salt to taste
1 cup young evening primrose leaves,
   torn to 1-inch pieces
½ cup evening primrose flowers
Fresh cracked pepper and salt to taste

Steam seedpods until tender (5–10 minutes) and allow them to cool.

In a large salad bowl, whisk together oil, vinegar, thyme, and salt. Toss cooled seedpods and leaves in vinegar mixture. Garnish with evening primrose flowers, adjust seasoning, and serve.

Honesty

Money Plant, Silver Dollars
Lunaria annua

This is one of those plants many of us remember from our childhoods. My brothers and sisters and I called them money plants because, throughout the winter, the nearly round seedpods shimmered a silvery-white in the sunlight. We occasionally used them for play money, so coming upon a laden plant was like finding a pot of gold, er, silver. Adults enjoyed them in a different way. My paternal grandma loved incorporating honesty in her dried flower arrangements, a tradition she passed down to me.

Honesty is an herbaceous biennial plant native to the Balkans and southwest Asia. It is naturalized throughout Europe, North America, and parts of Asia. It is a member of the brassica family, which includes broccoli, cabbage, kale, cauliflower, and brussels sprouts. The common name honesty arose in the 16th century, perhaps due to the seedpods being too translucent to conceal their seeds. In Denmark it is known as *Judaspenge* and in the Netherlands as *Judaspenning* ("coins of Judas"), a reference to the story of Judas Iscariot and the 30 pieces of silver he was paid.

Honesty has several phases for us to enjoy. The first year's growth is only about 6 inches high, but in the second year it rapidly shoots up to as high as 2 or 3 feet. Flower colors range from white to bright purple, quite a contrast from the usual yellow and white of most plants in the mustard family. Honesty is pollinated by bees, flies, butterflies, moths, and hummingbirds and is noted for attracting wildlife.

Honesty is easy to grow in the flower garden and makes a lovely, scented cut flower. Although not native to North America, honesty is not especially invasive. However, because it does escape its cultivated flower beds, it is monitored by agricultural specialists.

IN THE FIELD

What It Looks Like: Grows 2–4 feet high and about 1 foot in diameter. Plant is lightly branched, except near apex where flowering stems occur. Green or reddish stems have scattered long white hairs. Alternate leaves up to 3½ inches across (excluding petioles). Lower leaves of mature plants oval to heart shaped, sometimes almost triangular, coarsely serrated, with long hairy petioles (leaf stems) that are green or reddish purple. Upper leaves of mature plants somewhat smaller in size and lack stems. Basal leaves of young plants narrower than leaves of mature plants. Central stem and upper side stems terminate in 2- to 6-inch loose clusters of pleasantly scented flowers. Each flower about ¾ inch across with four pinkish-purple petals. Flowers bloom from early to late summer. In late August and early September each flower replaced by seedpod about 1–1½ inches long that is oval to round. As autumn progresses, seedpods (silicles) become papery and nearly white with age. Hardy and not frost tender.

Where to Find: Occurs throughout the United States, except Alabama, Florida, Georgia, Kansas, Louisiana, Mississippi, Nebraska, New Hampshire, North Carolina, North Dakota, Oklahoma, South Dakota, Texas, and Wyoming. Common at edges of woodlands, in hedges, and in semishaded areas of flower gardens. Grows in a variety of soil types, but prefers moist, loamy soils in full sun or light shade; grows poorly in acidic soils.

When to Harvest: Pick leaves beginning in April. Harvest flowers May through July. Collect young seedpods from late May until they become too tough to cook with. Seeds ripen from July to August.

What to Eat: Leaves, young seedpods, flowers, roots.

How to Harvest: Leaves, flowers, and seedpods are all easily gathered by hand. Collect roots with a stout trowel or shovel.

Poisonous Look-Alikes to Avoid: None.

IN THE KITCHEN

Why You Should Eat It: Full of phytochemicals and antioxidants; a powerful weapon in warding off many common diseases such as cancer, heart disease, diabetes, and hypertension.

What It Tastes Like: Broccoli, cabbage, mustard greens.

How to Store: Place leaves and/or seedpods in an airtight container with a damp paper towel; refrigerate up to a week. Use flowers immediately. Store root wrapped in moist paper towels in refrigerator for up to a week.

How to Cook: Eat leaves, flowers, and roots cooked or raw. Use seeds as a mustard-seed substitute; mustard flavor develops when cold water is added to ground-up seed—the reaction takes 10–15 minutes.

Honesty, Wild Pea, and Tofu Stir-Fry

I am fortunate enough to have several honesty plants in my front yard from which to pluck the young seedpods to add to stir-fries. Besides the novelty of serving something with such an unusual shape, cooking with the honesty plant adds a subtle note of mustard that works very well with other vegetables and meats.

* SERVES 4 *

3 tablespoons peanut oil

2 carrots, julienned to ¼ inch

4 scallions, cut in half, then sliced
   in two lengthwise

2 cups wild pea shoots, tough stems removed

1 cup young honesty seedpods

2 tablespoons fish sauce

3 tablespoons soy sauce

2 tablespoons toasted sesame seed oil

½ teaspoon crushed red chile peppers

8 ounces firm tofu, cut to ½-inch cubes

In a wok, heat oil on high. Just when oil begins to smoke, add carrots and scallions and toss to coat with oil. Stirring frequently, cook until carrots are slightly softened, about a minute. Add wild pea shoots and honesty. Toss until all is coated with oil. Add fish sauce, soy sauce, sesame seed oil, chile pepper, and tofu. Continue stirring frequently and cook just until all ingredients are heated through. Serve immediately.

Honesty Southwestern-Style

Most recipes you see for cooked greens and pork fall squarely under the 'Southern Style' heading. I've shifted this one to the Southwest, adding black beans, tomatoes, and extra garlic. The honesty seedpods provide a mild mustard flavor to this stew. Adjust the quantity of chicken broth for a heavier stew or to make soup, as desired.

* SERVES 4 *

½ pound bacon
1 Polish sausage or kielbasa,
  cut to 1-inch slices
2 16-ounce cans chicken broth
4 to 6 garlic cloves, pressed
2 cups young honesty seedpods
1 16-ounce can diced or whole tomatoes
1 16-ounce can black beans
Salt and pepper to taste

In a stockpot, fry bacon and sausage together. Remove sausage when browned. Continue frying bacon until crisp. Remove bacon from the pan, but leave bacon grease behind. Heat bacon grease on high heat until it is as hot as you can get it before it begins to smoke. Add chicken broth and garlic and bring to a boil. Reduce heat and simmer. Add honesty seedpods, tomatoes, beans, and sausages. Crumble bacon into the stockpot. Simmer on lowest setting for 10 minutes or until flavors are blended. Season to taste. Serve with rustic bread.

Honesty seedpods taste like mustard greens and add an interesting shape to stir-frys.

Japanese Knotweed

Bamboo Weed

Fallopia japonica, Polygonum cuspidatum, Reynoutria japonica

The 1990s marked a decade of serious flower gardening for me. I diligently ripped out large areas of turf in my front yard and replaced it with delphinium, peony, coreopsis, rose, alstromeria, nicotiana, penstemon, crocosmia, daylily, tradescantia, Asiatic lilies, and on and on. By the middle of the decade, I was so satisfied with the outcome in my front yard, I decided to do the same to the backyard. But first I would have to remove a gigantic patch of Japanese knotweed. I started in the wintertime, knocking all the dead and dried canes down and hauling them away. It was pretty easy work, and I remember feeling encouraged by this.

When spring came, an army of little red noses began poking up through the soil where I'd taken the canes down. My roommate, a professional landscaper, convinced me that we'd have to use Roundup on them before they got much of a start (see "Chemical Warfare" in chapter 1). He sprayed. And sprayed. And sprayed. All summer long. But the buds kept popping up. I nixed my plan to garden there and instead planted grass, then each summer we kept those little red noses mown short throughout the growing season. We didn't give them so much as a smidgeon of opportunity to photosynthesize. By year five of this treatment, the little red noses were still appearing but in greatly reduced numbers. Could I put a flower bed here? I decided not to risk it and kept the grass.

After nearly a decade, I moved from that lovely spot. It was very difficult to leave my flower beds behind—not so much the knotweed. Several years after leaving, I drove past the old place. There was the Japanese knotweed hedge, growing just as densely and tall as if I'd never touched the stuff! I sure wish I'd known it was edible. At least I could have experienced a bit of primal vindication by cooking and eating it!

Japanese knotweed is a large, very hardy, semi-woody perennial and a member of the Polygonaceae family, the same family that dock and rhubarb are in. The Polygonaceae family is also known as the knotweed, smartweed, or buckwheat family. The name Polygonaceae is derived from Greek for "many" (*poly*) and "knee" or "joint" (*goni*). Originating in Japan, this knotweed species is now widely considered to be an invasive species or weed in the United States and Europe. It is listed by the World Conservation Union as one of the world's 100 worst invasive species.

The success of the plant is partially due to its tolerance of a very wide range of soil types. Its rhizomes can survive temperatures of −31°F and can extend more than 20 feet horizontally and 10 feet deep, making removal by excavation extremely difficult. And as I mentioned above, the plant is very resilient to cutting, vigorously suckering back from the rhizomes. The invasive root system and strong growth can damage foundations, buildings, fences, roads, and retaining walls. Japanese knotweed is a frequent colonizer of roadsides and waste places as well as newly formed riverbanks. Because it forms thick, dense colonies, it tends to prevent many other herbaceous species from gaining a foothold.

On the plus side, the flowers are valued by many beekeepers as an important source of nectar at a time when little else is flowering, yielding a valued monofloral honey that northeastern US beekeepers fondly call bamboo honey. Also, organic farmers are looking at Japanese knotweed as potentially useful because its rhizomes contain a natural pesticide. Finally, in parts of Asia, the plant is known as *itadori*, which means "remove pain." It grows widely throughout Japan and is foraged as a wild vegetable (*sansai*).

Japanese knotweed is now considered one of the worst invasive exotics in parts of the eastern United States. It is listed as an invasive weed in Ohio, Vermont, Virginia, West Virginia, New York, Alaska, Pennsylvania, Oregon, and Washington.

IN THE FIELD

What It Looks Like: Stems stout, canelike, hollow between nodes, green with reddish mottled stripes, 5–8 feet tall, heavily branched. Stem joints or nodes swollen, surrounded by thin papery sheaths. Although plants die back in fall, dead canes typically persist throughout winter. Leaves thick and tough in texture, 2–7 inches long, about 1–5 inches wide, spade-shaped. One key characteristic is lack of hairs on leaves' undersides. Instead of hairs, slight bumplike structures called scabers along veins are visible with a magnifying glass. Flowers small, creamy white to greenish white, grow in showy, plumelike, branched clusters. Fruits three sided, shiny black.

Where to Find: Occurs throughout the United States, except Alabama, Arizona, Florida, Hawaii, Nevada, New Mexico, North Dakota, Texas, and Wyoming. Common along trails, roadsides, rivers, and streams as well as residential properties and associated green spaces. Tolerates partial shade; most competitive in moist, rich soil. Height often stunted on dry, exposed sites.

When to Harvest: Early spring.

What to Eat: Young shoots, young leaves, roots.

How to Harvest: Snip at ground level with scissors, garden snips, or a knife.

Poisonous Look-Alikes to Avoid: None.

IN THE KITCHEN

Why You Should Eat It: Provides potassium, phosphorus, zinc, and manganese. Contains respectable concentrations of quercetin, lysine, and resveratrol. Quercetin has antioxidant and antihistamine properties; lysine is an essential amino acid; resveratrol is good for heart health and is under study for its potential anti-aging properties (see Can Japanese Knotweed Prevent Heart Disease sidebar).

Who Should Avoid It: Contains oxalic acid, which can aggravate conditions such as rheumatism, arthritis, gout, kidney stones, or hyperacidity. If you suffer from any of these health conditions, consult your doctor prior to eating it (see Oxalic Acid sidebar in chapter 3). In addition, many people use herbicides on Japanese knotweed to try to control it. Before harvesting, check with the landowner about herbicide application.

What It Tastes Like: Tart flavor often compared to rhubarb. However, it doesn't taste exactly like rhubarb; has its own pleasant flavor profile.

How to Store: Shoots do not store well raw and begin to wither within a few hours; cook and refrigerate for several days or freeze. Dry roots for use in *itadori* tea.

How to Cook: Many Asian populations eat young shoots raw, and children consider them a treat. Also use as a substitute in any recipe calling for rhubarb. Remove outer skin with a vegetable peeler prior to eating or cooking. Slice stems and steam as a vegetable; simmer in soups, sauces, fruit compotes, and jam; or bake in desserts.

Can Japanese knotweed prevent heart disease?

Resveratrol is a chemical under study for preventing heart disease and cancer and extending life spans. It was originally extracted from the roots of hellebore in 1940. Then in 1963, it was isolated from the roots of Japanese knotweed. In 1992, scientists began to theorize that its presence in grape skins might explain red wine's beneficial effect on heart health.

Research on resveratrol is really in its infancy, but its potential effects are a topic of numerous animal and human studies. Though still debated by experts, it appears to benefit the life spans of fruit flies, nematode worms, fish, mice, and rats. There are also good indications it may prevent some types of cancer and lower blood sugar in lab mice.

The fact that resveratrol's potential benefit to humans remains largely unclear has not stood in the way of its growing popularity as an herbal supplement. With increasing demand, Japanese knotweed is now replacing grape by-products as the primary commercial source of resveratrol. Japanese knotweed is an important source of resveratrol, with concentrations even higher than those found in grape skins. Many resveratrol merchants now use Japanese knotweed and its scientific name in the supplement labels. Japanese knotweed is useful not just because its resveratrol concentration is high, but also because it's a very hardy plant and is easy to grow in many different climates. Human trials continue, with several already pointing to promising results.

Japanese Knotweed Chutney with Roast Pork Loin

This chutney is so easy to make. It's also simple to preserve for future feasts or gifts. I like it because it does not use as much vinegar as many other chutney recipes, my palate can better discern its complex flavors. This particular chutney also goes very well with lamb and goat roasts. Be forewarned: your chutney may have a greenish hue due to the knotweed, but I'm confident, and you should be too, that you won't mind that a bit once you've tasted it.

* SERVES 4 TO 6 *

ROAST PORK LOIN
- ⅛ cup brown sugar
- 1 teaspoon smoked paprika
- 1 teaspoon kosher salt
- ¼ teaspoon powdered ancho chile
- ½ teaspoon fresh black pepper
- ¼ teaspoon turmeric
- ¼ teaspoon coriander
- ½ teaspoon garlic powder
- ½ teaspoon cinnamon
- 1- to 1½-pound whole pork loin

CHUTNEY
- ½ cup golden raisins
- ½ cup hot water
- 2 tablespoons balsamic or red wine vinegar
- pinch of ground cloves
- pinch of ground nutmeg
- ½ cup sugar
- 2 shallots, finely chopped
- 2 tablespoons olive (or other vegetable) oil
- 1½ cups chopped fresh Japanese knotweed shoots, in ½-inch lengths
- salt and freshly ground pepper

Preheat oven to 550°F (or highest temperature). Use convection oven if you have it.

To prepare the pork loin, in a bowl combine brown sugar, paprika, salt, chile, black pepper, turmeric, coriander, garlic powder, and cinnamon. Rub into meat on all sides. Place spiced meat on a rack in a shallow roasting pan. Roast for 10 minutes. Turn down heat to 350°F and roast another 10–20 minutes, until a meat thermometer indicates the internal temperature has reached 145°F. Center of roast may be slightly pink.

Meanwhile, to make the chutney, in a bowl combine raisins, hot water, vinegar, cloves, nutmeg, and sugar. Let stand for at least 20 minutes.

In a medium saucepan, cook shallots in oil over medium heat until softened. Add raisin mixture and Japanese knotweed; season to taste. Cook uncovered on medium-low for 10–15 minutes, stirring frequently, until thickened.

To assemble this dish, remove roast pork loin from oven and let stand 5 minutes. Slice and serve with heaping spoonfuls of chutney.

Japanese Knotweed Muffins

If you've ever eaten apple or apricot muffins, you are familiar with that wonderful combination of moistness, sweetness, and tartness. Japanese knotweed muffins are similar. Once cooked, Japanese knotweed is usually not quite as sour as cooked rhubarb, and it makes an excellent addition to any dessert recipe calling for a tart fruit.

* MAKES 12 TO 18 MUFFINS *

TOPPING

1 teaspoon melted butter
1/3 cup brown sugar
1 teaspoon cinnamon

MUFFINS

2¼ cups whole wheat flour
1 cup brown sugar
1 teaspoon baking soda
1 teaspoon baking powder
½ cup oil
1 egg
1 teaspoon vanilla
1 cup buttermilk (or add 1 teaspoon vinegar or lemon juice to regular milk and let sit for 3 minutes)
1½ cups peeled and diced Japanese knotweed shoots, in ¾-inch pieces

Preheat oven to 400°F. In a bowl, mix melted butter, 1/3 cup brown sugar, and cinnamon; set topping aside.

In a large mixing bowl, combine flour, 1 cup brown sugar, baking soda, and baking powder. Separately, whisk together oil, egg, vanilla, and buttermilk. Make a shallow well in the dry ingredients with the back of a spoon. Pour liquids into the well and mix briefly. Stir in Japanese knotweed.

Fill 12 large or 18 small muffin tins to ¾ full. Sprinkle topping over muffins. Bake 15 minutes or until an inserted toothpick comes out clean.

OPPOSITE Collect Japanese knotweed before leaves fully emerge.

Pineapple Weed

Wild Chamomile, Disc Mayweed
Matricaria discoidea or *Matricaria matricarioides*

Goodness, I remember this as one of the first plants I ever picked. I had to be two or three years old, and this is one of the more vivid memories from my toddlerhood. My young parents didn't have a pot to piss in back then, and we lived in a dilapidated old house near Interstate 5 in Olympia, Washington. Our driveway was gravel and, like all children, I liked picking through the pebbles to see what sparkly treasures I might find. I remember being drawn to the sweet smell of the pineapple weeds that grew there, and I often picked and crushed the odd flowers. I'm sure I must have eaten a few too. How could an inquisitive toddler *not* put one of those flower heads in her mouth? They are, after all, the perfect nibbling size and shape for a small child to sample. I do not remember that my mother ever caught and cautioned me on the dangers of putting that particular plant in my mouth, though she did with many others during the course of my childhood. Maybe she knew, as I instinctively did at that age, that they were nothing to be concerned over.

Pineapple weed, an herbaceous annual plant in the Asteraceae family, is native to North America and northeast Asia. Some sources suggest it may have originally been brought to North America from Asia by Amerindians prior to European contact. Today, pineapple weed is also common in northern and western Europe.

The common name pineapple weed is probably more a reference to the plant's appearance than to its scent. When crushed, the flowers exude a sweet chamomile (some say pineapple) scent. The genus name *Matricaria* is derived from the Latin word *matrix*, which means "womb" or "mother."

Pineapple weed has been used for medicinal purposes for centuries, including for relief of gastrointestinal upset, infected sores, fevers, and postpartum anemia, but it can also be used as a food and flavoring agent. Containing chrysin, the same flavone that chamomile contains, pineapple weed tea is thought to provide the same calming effects as chamomile tea. Native Americans have treated headaches using pillows filled with dried pineapple weed. Herbalists sometimes administer a strong tea to bring a mother into her milk.

Besides its food and medicinal value, pineapple weed can be used as an effective insect repellent by rubbing it onto your skin. Although pineapple weed can spread in agricultural settings, it is not considered problematic.

IN THE FIELD

What It Looks Like: Typically grows 3–8 inches tall, though in perfect conditions can grow to 16 inches. When bruised, leaves and flower heads smell sweet, like chamomile. Leaves well branched, looking a bit like a miniature shrub. Fernlike leaves alternate along a hairless stem and are about ¾ inch wide and up to 2 inches long. Simple or compound leaves pinnately divided into linear lobes. Flower heads develop from nodes of upper leaves and are borne on stalks about ½–1½ inches long. Flower heads cone shaped or domed, sometimes compared to slightly used pencil erasers. Flowers consist of numerous greenish-yellow disk florets (no ray florets or petals). Flowers typically bloom from late spring through summer, sometimes into late autumn. Disk florets replaced by oblong fruits called achenes. Although achenes are without tufts of hairs, as a cluster they appear slightly hairy. Spreads by reseeding. Roots a branching taproot.

Where to Find: Occurs throughout the United States, except Alabama, Florida, Georgia, Hawaii, and Texas. Common in driveways and sidewalks, gravelly areas along railroads and roads, and gravelly, sunny vacant lots. Strongly prefers disturbed areas. Usually in full sun and gravelly or compacted soil. Does not flourish near taller plants.

When to Harvest: Flowers and leaves June through September.

What to Eat: Flowers, leaves.

How to Harvest: Easily gathered by hand.

Poisonous Look-Alikes to Avoid: None.

IN THE KITCHEN

Why You Should Eat It: Nutritional value unknown. Flower tea used as a mild sedative. Greatest value probably lies in its sweet flavor.

What It Tastes Like: Flowers and foliage often compared to chamomile or pineapple. Greens may become bitter after plant blooms.

How to Store: Well suited for drying.

How to Cook: Use young flower buds in salads or fresh or dried to make tea. Use in desserts for a delicate hint of chamomile or pineapple flavoring.

Pineapple Weed Cookies

I love adding flavors to simple sugar cookies. It's an easy way to turn a rather boring standard into something a bit exotic. Pineapple weed imparts a subtle fruitiness here—a cross between pineapple and chamomile. Samplers are likely to say, "It tastes so familiar, but I just can't put my finger on that lovely flavor."

* MAKES 1 DOZEN *

¼ cup fresh pineapple weed flowers
½ cup softened unsalted butter
1 cup sugar
2 eggs
½ teaspoon vanilla
1¾ cups flour
½ teaspoon salt

Preheat oven to 350°F. Coarsely chop pineapple weed blossoms and set aside.

Cream butter and sugar, then beat in eggs and vanilla. Fold in pineapple weed flowers. Combine with flour and salt. Drop by teaspoonfuls onto a lightly greased baking sheet. Bake for 10 minutes.

Pineapple Weed–Infused Whipped Cream with Baked Apricots and Roasted Almonds

....

Cream infusions are a novel way of further dressing up a fancy dessert. The hint of sweet pineapple weed cream is a great complement to the tart bite of a baked apricot. If you don't have (or don't like) almonds, chopped hazelnuts are an excellent substitution.

* SERVES 4 *

1 cup chilled heavy cream, divided
¼ cup fresh pineapple weed flowers
1 pound fresh apricots, halved, pits removed
3 tablespoons sugar, divided
3½ tablespoons butter
3 tablespoons almond slivers

Make infused cream several hours ahead of time: heat ½ cup cream in a small saucepan over medium heat until bubbles form around edges of pan. Remove pan from heat; add pineapple weed flowers. Let steep 20 minutes. Transfer to a medium bowl. Cover; chill until cold, about 2 hours.

A half hour before dessert is to be served, preheat oven to 400°F and generously butter a large baking dish, using about ½ tablespoon. Put apricot halves, cut side up in one layer, in the prepared baking dish. Sprinkle with 2 tablespoons sugar, dot with remaining 3 table-spoons of butter, and bake until tender, about 15 minutes or until apricots are caramelized with sugar but still retain their shape.

Meanwhile, strain infused cream through a fine-mesh sieve into a medium bowl. Add remaining ½ cup cream and 1 tablespoon sugar. Using an electric mixer, beat cream until soft peaks form.

Roast almond slivers in a small skillet over medium heat for 3–4 minutes, stirring frequently.

To serve, place several warm or room-temperature apricots in each of four dessert dishes, top with whipped cream, and sprinkle with roasted almond slivers.

Sow Thistle

Common Sow Thistle, Field Milk Thistle
Sonchus oleraceus

My husband, Carlos, teaches green engineering at Seattle University on Seattle's Capitol Hill. The lovely campus grounds feature all manner of beautiful plant life. Ciscoe Morris of Seattle's locally televised "Gardening with Ciscoe" was the groundskeeper there for a number of years, and left behind many unusual plantings.

If you knew my husband, you would know that it makes complete sense that, of all the lovely plants to feast his eyes upon, his attention fell one day to a humble patch of sow thistle near the parking garage. Just before it began to flower, he brought home a sizable harvest.

I had used it in the past in stir-fries and as a steamed vegetable, but we hadn't yet tried it raw. Although Carlos's cache was already a couple feet tall, it was young and tender. He tore a leaf off and sampled it. "It is good," he announced as he handed me a leaf of my own.

I had to agree: it had a mild, nonbitter flavor and the texture was tender but hearty, almost succulent to the touch. While I enjoy steaming and stir-frying wild greens, I get downright excited when we discover something new that works fresh in a salad.

"I'll just start bringing some home every afternoon after class," Carlos offered. I was only too happy to encourage him. While the leaves were still young, we used them as a salad green and, after they flowered, as a stir-fry ingredient.

I wonder what his students thought when they saw Carlos stooping to pick weeds and hauling them off to the back of his car. Did they believe he was helping with the weeding, or was he just another eccentric professor behaving strangely?

We also had a brief discussion on the pronunciation of sow thistle. Carlos's mouth turns it into "sow sistle." I corrected him one time too many and he asked me, "Would you rather I pronounce it 'thow thithle'?" Since then, our household calls it "thow thithtle."

Sonchus is a genus of flowering plants in the daisy family, Asteraceae. Most of these species are annual herbs, but there are also a few perennials; common sow thistle (*Sonchus oleraceus*) is an annual. Native to Europe, Asia, and Africa, it is now found almost worldwide in temperate regions. Because sow thistle exudes a milky latex when cut, the plants were once fed to lactating sows with the notion that the mothers' milk production would increase for healthier piglets—hence the common name.

All *Sonchus* species are edible and have been valuable food plants to a wide variety of cultures throughout human history. In ancient times, sow thistle enjoyed an excellent reputation as a food plant and a medicine; and sow thistle is still used in Europe as a potherb. Italians commonly cook it in traditional pasta dishes. Healthy Cretans, many of whom live to a ripe old age, include it in their traditional dish *Horta Vrasta* (see Horta Vrasta sidebar in chapter 4). In New Zealand, it's known as *puha* or *rareki* and is frequently eaten as a vegetable, particularly by the native Maori, who also use the milky sap as a chewing gum.

Sadly, in spite of all its popularity elsewhere, the United States considers it a noxious weed in many regions because it has the unacceptable habit of popping up in agricultural fields, it grows quickly in a wide range of conditions, it spreads rapidly by seed, and few Americans know of its edibility.

IN THE FIELD

What It Looks Like: Stem hollow; stems and leaves exude milky sap when cut. Leaves bluish-green, hairless, lacking a stalk, tapering at the base to clasp the stem. Leaves are soft and lanceolate to somewhat irregularly lobed, forming a basal rosette in their immature stage. Plant bolts in midspring, with plants reaching up to 4–5 feet in height depending on growing conditions. Plant color ranges from green to gray to purplish in older specimens. Flower heads, comprised of several yellow florets with fringed petals, range ½–1 inch in diameter. Yellow flowers resemble those of dandelion. Globular white seed heads also similar to but smaller than the dandelion's.

Where to Find: Occurs throughout the United States, except Alabama, Arizona, Arkansas, Florida, Georgia, Hawaii, Oklahoma, and South Carolina. Found in vacant lots, roadsides, and disturbed soils. Prefers full sun and moist soil, but can tolerate shade and most soil conditions.

When to Harvest: Early spring to late fall.

What to Eat: Leaves, stems, roots.

How to Harvest: Fine to collect entire plant; however, collecting just younger leaves allows plant to continue to produce leaves for future harvesting. Pinching off any blooms also increases yield.

Poisonous Look-Alikes to Avoid: None; all sow thistles edible, though *Sonchus oleraceus* considered the best.

IN THE KITCHEN

Why You Should Eat It: Similar to dandelion; excellent source of vitamins A and C, thiamine, riboflavin, niacin, calcium, phosphorus, and iron.

What It Tastes Like: Young leaves taste much like lettuce. Some say cooked greens remind them of chard or spinach. Older leaves and stalks can be somewhat bitter but generally still palatable, especially if cooked.

How to Store: Place leaves with a damp paper towel in a loosely closed plastic bag in refrigerator crisper for up to a week.

How to Cook: Cook peeled stems like asparagus. Can eat young roots cooked, though not a common practice. Boil or steam leaves, add to soups, sauté, or stir-fry.

Sow thistle blooms in clusters of composite flowers that look a lot like dandelion flowers.

Sow Thistle Omelet

Here's a flavorful carb cutter that not only makes an easy, delicious morning starter, but is substantial enough to satisfy even a lunch or light dinner appetite.

* SERVES 4 *

4 eggs
2 cups coarsely chopped sow thistle leaves, stems, and flowers—remove any tough stalks
¹/₈ cup feta cheese
½ teaspoon onion powder
¼ teaspoon ground nutmeg
Salt and pepper to taste
2 tablespoons olive oil

In a medium-size bowl, beat eggs. Stir in sow thistle and feta cheese. Season with onion powder, nutmeg, salt, and pepper.

Heat olive oil in a small skillet over medium heat. Add the egg mixture and cook about 3 minutes, until partially set. Flip with a spatula. Reduce heat to low and continue cooking 2–3 minutes or to desired doneness. Serve immediately.

Sow Thistle Sautéed with Pancetta

This recipe is inspired by Southern-made collard greens, but I've dressed it up a tad with pancetta, garlic, wine, raisins, and nuts and omitted any boiling to retain more of the nutritional value. As with all good sautés, this one is simple, straightforward, and irresistibly good.

* SERVES 4 *

½ medium to large red onion, sliced to ¼ inch thick
2 tablespoons olive oil
4 ounces pancetta (or other salted pork, ham, sausage, etc.), sliced to 1-inch pieces
2 cloves garlic, coarsely chopped
½ teaspoon sea salt
4 cups sow thistle leaves, loosely packed
¼ cup white wine
¼ cup raisins
¼ cup coarsely chopped hazelnuts (or other nuts)

In a wok or large pan, cook onion in olive oil on high until soft. Add pancetta, garlic, and salt; cook for 1–2 minutes, stirring frequently. Add sow thistle, wine, raisins, and nuts. Cook just until greens are wilted, about a minute. Adjust salt to taste. Serve alone or over rice, grain, or pulse of your choice.

Wild Fennel

Sweet Fennel, Common Fennel
Foeniculum vulgare

think Seattle might be the Wild Fennel Capital of the World. No kidding; you can drive down several of the interstates that intersect my city and find intermittent patches of wild fennel that stretch literally for miles. A plant that originates from an arid climate, fennel seems to *love* living in the dry, dusty cracks of pavement and cement, which I guess should come as no surprise. Highways are usually underlain with crushed, packed drain rock—apparently a terrain similar enough to fennel's native Mediterranean.

For many years I thought this plant was wild dill, as they closely resemble one another when you're driving down the freeway at 70 miles per hour. While I like dill, it is not nearly as enticing to me as the licorice flavor of fennel. The vegetable we often see labeled fennel in our grocery stores is a more mildly flavored species known as finocchio. Its swollen, bulblike stem is used in Mediterranean cuisine such as salads, pastas, and risottos.

One night I planned a salmon dinner and realized I was out of dill. No matter, I thought, I'll just drive a half mile down Old Highway 99 and fetch some. (I don't usually collect near busy roads but will occasionally do so in a pinch.) I had mixed feelings on learning that all those feathery fronds were actually fennel, not dill. While I love it, licorice was not the flavor I was seeking for my salmon bake. But with dinnertime approaching, I decided on wild fennel as a yet untested (for me) substitute—one that I hoped my poor guinea pig friends wouldn't mind taste testing. I probably don't have to tell you that we all savored the switch, and I've since made the dish that way many times.

Wild fennel is an aromatic, herbaceous perennial plant with feathery leaves and yellow flowers arranged in umbels.

It's native to the Mediterranean region but is naturalized in much of the rest of the world. Like the anise plant, fennel is in the Apiaceae family, and both share a flavor similar to licorice (although licorice is actually in the legume family). The word fennel comes from the Latin word for "hay," *feniculum* or *foeniculum*.

Wild fennel's culinary and medicinal use in Europe probably originated in Greece and spread through the expansion of the Roman Empire. Judging from *Apicius*, the only surviving classical cookbook of the Roman Empire, wild fennel was common to ancient Roman cooking. Ancient Rome regarded wild fennel as the herb of sight, and today several cultures eat raw fennel seeds to improve eyesight. Arab traders probably helped spread wild fennel's use to the Middle East, India, and China.

In medieval times, wild fennel seeds were used by King Edward as an appetite suppressant. Later, Puritans used them during long church services, leading to their reference as "meetin' seeds."

Today, fennel is widely cultivated for its edible, flavorful achenes (seedlike fruits containing seeds). The plant's anise flavor comes from anethole, the same aromatic compound that gives anise and star anise their flavor. The foliage and seeds of the wild fennel plant are used in many of the culinary traditions of the world. Fennel pollen is the most cherished form of fennel among great chefs, but also the most expensive. Fennel seed is a common ingredient in Italian sausages and meatballs as well as northern European rye breads. It's also found in foods from China, India, Pakistan, Afghanistan, Iran, and Lebanon.

Wild fennel is a common agricultural weed typically controlled with applications of glyphosate (Roundup).

IN THE FIELD

What It Looks Like: Entire plant is light green, grows to heights of up to 8 feet with hollow stems. Leaves grow up to 2 feet long, finely dissected (fernlike), with smallest segments nearly threadlike; leaves similar to those of dill. Flowers produced in umbels 2–5 inches wide at ends of stems, each umbel section having 20–50 small, individual yellow flowers. Fruits narrow, from a little over ⅛ inch to more than ⅜ inch long, grooved and seed shaped. Not frost tender; hardy to USDA zone 5.

Where to Find: Occurs throughout the United States, except Alabama, Arkansas, Colorado, Idaho, Indiana, Minnesota, Montana, New Hampshire, North Dakota, Oklahoma, South Dakota, Vermont, and Wyoming. Common in full sun in well-drained meadows, cultivated beds, wastelands, habitat margins, roadsides, and cracks in pavement and concrete sidewalks. Prefers well-drained sandy, loamy, or clay soil. Drought tolerant.

When to Harvest: Leaves best collected in early spring, but younger growth can be harvested all summer. Stems collected in late summer, fruits in fall and early winter. Collect pollen by shaking each flower gently into a bag.

What to Eat: Stems, flowers, fruits, leaves.

How to Harvest: Collect fruits and foliage by hand. Heavier stems require shears or snips. Most flavorful fruits are those nearest center of each umbel.

Poisonous Look-Alikes to Avoid: When collecting wild fennel, take special care to avoid confusing it with two deadly poisonous plants, poison hemlock and water hemlock. A useful test to distinguish between hemlock and fennel is to crush some of the leaves and smell them. Fennel smells like anise or licorice, whereas poison hemlock's smell is often described as mouselike or musty. See chapter 6, Poisonous Weeds Common to Urban Areas, for more information.

IN THE KITCHEN

Why You Should Eat It: Good source of vitamin A, potassium, calcium, and phosphorus. Extracts of fennel seed have been shown in animal studies to have a potential use in the treatment of glaucoma. There is also growing clinical evidence that fennel may be an effective diuretic and a potential drug for treatment of hypertension. Clinical studies have shown that fennel, as part of the diet, helps regulate contractions of the small intestine and aids gas expulsion. Fennel also relaxes the gut, which can relieve spasms of the gastrointestinal tract. As a result, fennel is used in the management of irritable bowel symptoms. Fennel is also a traditional digestive aid for colic, heartburn, indigestion, and stomachaches. Finally, fennel has antioxidant and antimicrobial properties.

Who Should Avoid It: There are potential problems for some with ingestion of concentrated fennel oil found in health food stores.

What It Tastes Like: Dried fennel fruits taste like licorice or anise. Green fruits are strongly flavored; best as a cooking spice. Leaves milder than the fruits. Fennel fairly strong when raw; cooking mellows and sweetens the flavor.

How to Store: To maintain freshness for two or three days, place stems in a vase with a couple inches of water, or store between damp paper towels in refrigerator. Keep dried seeds in an airtight container for a year or longer.

How to Cook: Use fennel fronds and young stems to flavor many different sweet and savory dishes. Fennel seed works well in roasted, grilled, sautéed, or braised dishes. Boiling and steaming tend to reduce its intensity. Fennel seed is commonly used with fish, sausage, pickles, breads, and fruit. Fennel fronds are great in salads; add to soups and stews just before serving.

Wild Fennel Cookies

I often use wild fennel when I want to add a subtle licorice flavor. This recipe is a combination of an Italian comfort food, anisette cookies, and an American comfort food, sugar cookies. If you prefer a stronger licorice or anise flavoring, you can double the fennel quantity without harming the recipe.

* MAKES 2 DOZEN *

½ cup butter
1½ cup sugar, divided
1 egg
¼ cup wild fennel fronds, finely chopped
1¾ cups flour
1½ teaspoons baking powder
¼ teaspoon salt
½ teaspoon wild fennel seed, ground

Preheat oven to 350°F. In a large bowl, cream butter and 1 cup sugar until light and fluffy. Add egg and beat to combine. Add wild fennel fronds.

In a small bowl, stir together flour, baking powder, and salt. Stir dry ingredients into butter mixture one-third at a time. With your hands, shape dough into 1½-inch balls and place on lightly greased baking sheet.

In a small bowl, mix ground wild fennel seed with remaining ½ cup sugar. Dip the bottom of a glass in water, then into the sugar mixture. Gently flatten each cookie using the bottom of the coated glass. Bake cookies for 8–10 minutes or until very lightly browned and puffed. Remove cookies from pan immediately.

Wild Fennel and Bibb Lettuce Salad

I like using bibb lettuce for this salad because its sweet and mild flavor allows wild fennel's lovely flavor and scent to really shine through. For the most aromatic, heavenly kiss of fennel, serve this salad immediately after you've added freshly chopped fronds.

* SERVES 4 TO 6 *

¼ cup red wine vinegar
¼ cup sugar
½ teaspoon salt
¼ cup olive oil
2 roasted red bell peppers, halved
   and sliced thinly
2 small heads Boston bibb lettuce
   ("butter lettuce"), or 1 large head,
   coarsely chopped
1 cup coarsely chopped wild fennel fronds
2 tangerines, peeled, pith and seeds
   removed, and segmented
½ red onion, thinly sliced

In a large salad bowl, whisk vinegar, sugar, and salt together. Set aside until sugar and salt are fully dissolved. Whisk in oil. Toss peppers, lettuce, fennel fronds, tangerines, and onion with dressing. Serve immediately.

Above the lowly plants it towers,
The fennel, with its yellow flowers,
And in an earlier age than ours
Was gifted with the wondrous powers,
Lost vision to restore.
It gave new strength, and fearless mood;
And gladiators, fierce and rude,
Mingled it in their daily food;
And he who battled and subdued,
A wreath of fennel wore.

—Henry Wadsworth Longfellow
from *The Goblet of Life*

Wild Mustard

Hedge Mustard, Singer's Plant, Tumbling Mustard, Oriental Mustard,
Oriental Rocket, English Watercress
Sisymbrium officinale

arly on, I had trouble keeping up with this plant's everchanging appearance. It's a regular master of disguises. When it first pops up in early spring, it's lush with grass-green leaves and can look almost like a small shrub. But by the end of June, the leaves virtually disappear and the remaining cluster of wiry stems looks more like a tumbleweed. In the Pacific Northwest, wild mustard arrives as early as late February; thus my advice is to start sleuthing for them very early so as not to miss out on a flavorful leafy green.

Wild mustard is an herbaceous annual plant (sometimes biennial in milder climates) native to southern Europe now well established in most parts of the world, from Asia and Africa to North America. Though in the Brassicaceae (cabbage) family, it is not classified within the *Brassica* (mustard) genus. The genus name *Sisymbrium* is derived from the Latinized Greek word *sisumbrion*, which means "aromatic herb."

In addition to being edible, wild mustard is credited with a number of medicinal uses. The ancient Greeks believed wild mustard was an antidote to all poisons. Tibetans still use it as a medicine to repress the symptoms of food poisoning. In folk medicine, it was known as singer's plant as it was used to soothe sore throats. Today, herbalists use the plants to treat bronchitis and stomach ailments and as a revitalizer.

Throughout much of Europe, the plant is cultivated for its leaves and seeds and it is used as a condiment in Denmark, Norway, Germany, and other parts of northern Europe. Here in the United States, we are busily trying to rid our fields and gardens of the stuff. It is considered weedy or invasive in numerous states. As a side note, wild mustard can be used as a soil conditioner because its roots secrete an alkaline substance that helps sweeten acidic soil.

IN THE FIELD

What It Looks Like: Grows to 3 feet tall by about a foot in diameter; occasionally grows to 6 feet tall. Though lush and leafy in spring and early summer, becomes like a small tumbleweed by mid- to late summer. Plant grows from a taproot, first forming a basal rosette followed by flowering stalks with alternate leaves. Stems light green to purplish green, branching occasionally to abundantly. Basal and lower leaves up to 8 inches long, 2 inches across; upper leaves up to 4 inches long, 1½ inches across. Leaves green and hairless, pinnate, deeply lobed, with backward or spreading segments. Upper stems terminate in long (up to 10 inches), slender clusters of yellow flowers. Flowers also produced at nodes of upper leaves. Each flower a little less than ¼ inch across with four yellow petals. Fruits (seedpods) called siliques are less than an inch long, narrow and straight to slightly curved cylinders, light brown at maturity; each silique splits in half to release several seeds. Small seeds short, cylindrical, slightly flattened, reddish brown, about $\frac{1}{32}$ inch in length. A hermaphrodite: self-fertile. Spreads by reseeding. Not frost tender.

Where to Find: Occurs throughout the United States. Found on roadsides and wasteland, among rubble, woodland borders, degraded meadows, fields and pastures, barnyards, poorly maintained gardens, along railroads. Prefers full to partial sun, moist to slightly dry conditions, and fertile, loamy soil with a high level of nitrogen. However, readily adapts to other kinds of soil; soil fertility and moisture conditions influence plant size.

When to Harvest: Gather leaves in spring. Flowers available June to July; seeds ripen in July and August.

What to Eat: Leaves, flowers, seed.

How to Harvest: Easily harvest leaves by hand in spring. Stems become wiry later in season; use snips to remove flower racemes and seeds.

Poisonous Look-Alikes to Avoid: None.

IN THE KITCHEN

Why You Should Eat It: Information unavailable, but most plants in the Brassicaceae family are high in phytonutrients that protect against various cancers.

Who Should Avoid It: Leaves very effective at collecting road dust and also quite adept at taking up heavy metals, so avoid collecting near busy roads or other polluted places.

What It Tastes Like: Leaves taste somewhere between cabbage, broccoli, and mustard greens.

How to Store: Keep loosely wrapped leaves and flowers in refrigerator for several days. Dry seeds and store for up to a year in sealed containers.

How to Cook: Use raw in salads or cooked as a potherb. Eat young shoots raw or cooked. Eat seeds raw or cooked, or grind into powder and use as a gruel or a mustard condiment.

Wild Mustard Greens Southern-Style

Thinking about Southern barbecued ribs for dinner tonight? Here is a fitting and hearty side dish for you. Wild mustard substitutes for store-bought mustard greens, leaf for leaf. For a stand-alone meal, I serve these greens with johnny cakes (cornmeal pancakes).

* SERVES 4 *

½ pound ham hock
2 quarts water
1 onion, diced
1½ cups cooked black-eyed peas
4 cups packed wild mustard greens
vinegar and/or Tabasco sauce to taste

In a 3-quart soup pot over medium heat, boil ham hock in about 2 quarts of water for an hour or until meat is tender enough to fall off the bone. Remove bones, leaving meat and pot liquor behind. Reduce heat to a simmer. Add greens and cook over low heat until tender, about 5 minutes. Add black-eyed peas to greens. Drain, reserving pot liquor to spoon over the dish. Season to taste with vinegar and/or Tabasco sauce.

Wild Mustard Greens Stir-Fried with Tofu

When we go out for Chinese dim sum, I always get a couple small plates of mustard greens. This recipe is a bit spicier than what I've had in restaurants, and I've also added tofu to the mix to bump up the protein content. If you're not a tofu fan, the recipe works just as well without it.

* SERVES 4 *

1 tablespoon rice vinegar

2 tablespoons soy sauce

½ teaspoon sugar

1 pound wild mustard greens, stems removed

1 12-ounce package extra-firm tofu, cut into ½-inch cubes

¼ cup plus 1 tablespoon peanut oil

1 shallot, coarsely chopped

1-inch piece fresh ginger, coarsely chopped

2 cloves garlic, coarsely chopped

1 teaspoon wine or sherry

1 tablespoon toasted sesame seeds

Collect spear-shaped mustard leaves while they're young; by mid-summer the plant loses its leaves and resembles a tumbleweed.

Mix vinegar, soy sauce, and sugar together; set aside.

Steam mustard greens 3–5 minutes; drain and set aside.

In a wok, fry tofu in small batches in ¼ cup peanut oil. Drain tofu and set aside.

Add 1 tablespoon peanut oil to the hot wok. Add shallot, ginger, and garlic; stir-fry about a minute, taking care not to burn them. Stir in wine. Add greens to wok and cook about a minute, until wilted. Add soy sauce–vinegar mixture and stir-fry 1–2 minutes, mixing well. Add tofu and stir a few times just until reheated. Add sesame seeds and stir to combine well. Serve with brown rice.

Wild Pea

Perennial Sweet Pea, Everlasting Pea, Pea Vine
Lathyrus latifolius

n my early 20s, I lived next door to a quarter-mile-long hedge of wild pea located on city-owned property. By mid-July, the hedge was a solid wall of varying hues of pink, lavender, and white. I loved filling my small apartment with bouquets of these colorful gifts from my nearby patch of urban nature. I would like to say that my living quarters were bathed in sweet-pea perfume, but unlike the annual we grow in our gardens, wild pea does not carry a sweet scent, or really much scent at all. No matter; they're quite beautiful to look at, and they make a very nice cut flower arrangement. Once again, I sure wish I'd known they were edible in those early days of endless ramen noodle dinners.

Wild pea is a perennial herbaceous vine. The genus name *Lathyrus* is derived from the Greek word for pea, *lathuros.* The species name *latifolius* is from the Latin word for "wide," lati, and "leaf," *folius,* which refers to its winged stems.

Wild pea has a wide natural distribution in southern and central Europe and into North Africa and has become naturalized in many countries worldwide. Like clover and other legumes, it's a nitrogen fixer—that is, it takes in atmospheric nitrogen, adding it to the surrounding soil and improving very poor soil. It can climb to 6 feet or more by means of twining tendrils, but in open areas it sprawls.

Wild pea has a long history as a garden plant and is grown commercially as a cut flower in Japan. This is a lovely plant for covering up outbuildings and fences. It can be quite weedy, but it is not especially difficult to control. While it lacks scent, it's quite beautiful and makes the perfect vine for covering up outbuildings and fences. Having just installed a fence in my front yard, I plan to grow my own beautiful mounds of wild peas this summer.

IN THE FIELD

What It Looks Like: Often climbs to 6 feet or more; in open areas more likely to creep along the ground, forming sprawling mounds. Winged, hairless stems produce alternating green compound leaves consisting of a single pair of leaflets and a winged stem about 2 inches long. Leaflets oval, smooth along edges, hairless, up to 3 inches long and 1 inch across. Branching tendrils form between leaflets. Short clusters of four to eleven flowers produced at leaf nodes. Flowers about ¾–1 inch across with five magenta-pink petals of same general shape as other flowers in the pea family. Blooms occur in July and August with color ranging between white, pink, and magenta. Unlike annual varieties, perennial sweet pea is nearly fragrance free. Peas develop from July through September, when flowers are replaced by hairless, flattened, green peapods, about 2 inches long and ½ inch wide, with eight to 12 green peas inside. Pods gradually turn brown, then suddenly split open, flinging seeds before the two pod halves spiral inward. At this stage, seeds are rather hard and gray to brown. Foliage fades and looks bedraggled by end of summer. Reproduces vegetatively from its taproot and rhizomes or by reseeding. Frost hardy, long-lived, slow spreading.

Where to Find: Occurs throughout the United States except Florida and North Dakota. Found in alleys, on chain-link fences, in roadsides, vacant lots, fields, embankments. Grows in many conditions, but usually found in dry, sunny locations.

When to Harvest: Pick young greens and flower buds in May and June. Gather flowers in late June and July. Harvest peas in August and September.

What to Eat: Flower buds, flowers, shoots, tendrils, seeds.

How to Harvest: Tender upper flowers, buds, and tendrils easily snap off the vine, leaving tougher counterparts behind.

Poisonous Look-Alikes to Avoid: Garden sweet pea (*Lathyrus odoratus*) can be toxic (see below). The two species can easily be distinguished because *Lathyrus odoratus* is heavily scented and *Lathyrus latifolius* is nearly scentless.

IN THE KITCHEN

Why You Should Eat It: Nutritional information unavailable, but it is likely high in protein. If wild peas are anything like garden varieties, whose wild ancestor is unknown, they are a good source of protein, vitamin A, riboflavin, niacin, vitamin B6, folate, magnesium, phosphorus, and copper and a very good source of dietary fiber, vitamin C, vitamin K, thiamin, and manganese.

Who Should Avoid It: Some species in this genus contain a toxic amino acid that can damage the nervous system. This disease, called lathyrism, only occurs when those species are frequently eaten in large amounts; small quantities are said to be nutritious. While no records of toxicity have been found for *Lathyrus latifolius,* some caution is advised and they should be eaten only in moderation and not daily. Having said this, I've eaten perennial sweet peas for several days in a row with absolutely no problem.

What It Tastes Like: Greens taste much like snap peas. Flower buds taste similarly but have an added flowery note not unlike orange blossom water. Peas taste very much like regular garden peas.

How to Store: Dry peas for future use. Store flower buds and greens between damp paper towels in refrigerator for one to two days. Use blossoms immediately.

How to Cook: Steam or boil peas. Eat buds, tendrils, and flowers raw in salads, lightly steamed, sautéed, or stir-fried. All plant parts lose color during cooking.

Wild Pea Shoots and Tendrils with Langostino

·······································

I like using langostino when I can find it because it's considered a solidly sustainable shellfish, not to mention it's just as yummy as lobster. Adding wild pea shoots and tendrils is a relatively new food fashion we now see regularly in fancier restaurants. Adding them to any dish lends a distinctly flowery flavor as well as visual appeal.

∗ SERVES 4 ∗

4 tablespoons butter
2 cloves garlic, minced
2 tablespoons grated fresh ginger
2 tablespoons dry white wine
1 pound fresh wild pea shoots, older stems discarded
2 tablespoons heavy cream
1 pound precooked shelled langostinos
Salt to taste

In a large skillet, melt butter over low heat. Add garlic and ginger; cook 1–2 minutes. Increase heat to medium. Add wine, pea shoots, and cream; cook uncovered until pea shoots are wilted, 1–2 minutes. Add langostinos and heat through. Salt to taste and serve immediately.

Wild Pea Shoots Stir-Fried with Garlic

Wild pea vines contrast nicely with garlic, rice wine, and tamari. I make this dish often because it's really simple and quick, and there are never any leftovers. The frequency with which we enjoy wild pea shoots is possible only because whenever I spot them from my car, I slam on the brakes and hang a U-turn to gather the evening's side dish.

* SERVES 4 *

1 tablespoon rice wine
¼ cup vegetable or chicken broth
2 teaspoon tamari or soy sauce
¼ teaspoon sugar
1 teaspoon cornstarch
2 teaspoons cold water
1 pound wild pea shoots
2 tablespoons peanut (or other vegetable) oil
4 cloves garlic, coarsely chopped

In a bowl, combine rice wine, broth, tamari, and sugar; set aside.

Mix cornstarch with cold water; set aside.

Remove and discard any heavy stems from pea shoots.

Heat oil in a wok over high heat. Add garlic and stir-fry just until fragrant, taking care not to burn it. Add pea shoots and stir to combine. Add sauce mixture; cover and cook until pea vines are tender, 1–2 minutes. Uncover. Add cornstarch mixture; cook while stirring just until sauce thickens. Serve with brown rice or a cooked hearty grain such as spelt or barley.

Young wild pea pods can be eaten raw or cooked just as you would snow peas.

Nine delicious ways to use wild pea shoots

1. Toss raw with lemon juice, truffle oil, and other greens for a light salad.
2. Stir-fry with garlic and sesame oil.
3. Use in omelets, frittatas, or quiches.
4. Add to soups just before serving.
5. Mix with pastas.
6. Use as a beautiful, edible garnish.
7. Lightly steam.
8. Eat raw as a snack.
9. Add to yakisoba or ramen recipes.

Edible flowers

Add flavor and color to your foraged meals with these edible flowers:

Arugula
Bee balm
Borage
Calendula
Carnation
Chamomile
Chives
Chrysanthemum
Cornflower
Bachelor's button
Dandelions (see chapter 2,
  Lawns and Parking Strips)
Daylily (see chapter 3, Vegetable
  Gardens and Flower Beds)

Dill
English daisy
Fennel
Fuchsia
Gardenia
Gladiolus
Hibiscus
Hollyhock
Honeysuckle
Impatiens
Lavender
Lilac
Mallow (see chapter 2,
  Lawns and Parking Strips)

Marigold
Nasturtium
Pansy
Primrose
Radish
Rose (see chapter 3,
  Vegetable Gardens
  and Flower Beds)
Snapdragon
Squash blossom
Sunflower
Tuberous begonia
Violet

But avoid these toxic blooms:

Azalea
Crocus
Daffodil
Foxglove
Garden sweet peas

Jack-in-the-pulpit
Lily of the valley
Oleander
Rhododendron
Wisteria

6 | POISONOUS WEEDS COMMON TO URBAN AREAS

Eating poisonous plants—and so absorbing toxins—is not uncommon, especially for children; poisonous plant ingestion accounts for more than 63,000 calls per year to national poison centers. However, only a few plants—poison hemlock and water hemlock included—are toxic to a life-threatening degree. Less than 20 percent of poisonous plant exposures require medical management. Still why risk it? This chapter describes toxic weeds commonly found in urban areas to help you avoid unpleasant or dangerous encounters.

Bittersweet

Nightshade, Deadly Nightshade

Solanum dulcamara

What It Looks Like: Semiwoody herbaceous perennial vine capable of reaching heights of 12–15 feet, though more often found at 3–6 feet high. Leaves 1½–5 inches long, roughly arrowhead-shaped, often lobed at the base. Flowers in loose clusters of 3 to 20, ½–1 inch across, star-shaped, with five purple petals and forward-pointing yellow stamens. Fruit a slightly oval, soft, juicy red berry about ½ inch long with appearance of a tiny tomato.

Why You Should Avoid It: All parts of the plant, including the fruit, contain alkaloids that are mildly poisonous. Ingestion can result in nausea, vomiting, and diarrhea. Large quantities can cause paralysis of the central nervous system, slow heart rate and respiration, low temperature, vertigo, delirium, convulsions, and death. Though regarded by most as a poisonous plant, bittersweet nightshade has a long history of a wide variety of medicinal uses.

Some sources confuse this species with *Atropa belladonna* because the two plants share the common name "deadly nightshade." All parts of *A. belladonna* are extremely toxic.

Creeping Buttercup

Ranunculus repens

What It Looks Like: Herbaceous perennial that spreads primarily by stolons. Grows to 20 inches tall; has both prostrate stems, which root at the nodes, as well as erect flowering stems. Shallowly to deeply lobed leaves divided into three broad, white-spotted, dark green leaflets up to 3 inches long. Leaves higher on stems are smaller, with narrower leaflets. Leaves and stems both finely hairy. Flowers bright golden yellow, often convex (cup-shaped), ³/₁₆–¼ inch in diameter, usually with five petals. Fruits are clusters of achenes ¹/₁₆–⅛ inch long. Grows in fields and pastures; prefers wet soil.

Why You Should Avoid It: Buttercup (and all plants in the ranunculus family) contains several alkaloids and glycosides; all parts of this plant are poisonous when raw. It also has a strongly acrid juice that can cause the skin to blister. Poisoning is rare because the acrid flavor prevents most people from consuming more than a bite. The toxins are destroyed by drying or heating, so some people enjoy eating the cooked greens. I have not tried this; if you wish to cook with it, work with someone who has a tried-and-true system.

Field Bindweed

Morning Glory

Convolvulus arvensis

What It Looks Like: Climbing or creeping herbaceous vine growing 20 inches to more than 6 feet high. Leaves spirally arranged, linear to arrowhead-shaped, ¾–2 inches long, alternate, with a ⅜- to 1-inch petiole. Flowers trumpet-shaped, ⅜–1 inch in diameter, white or pale pink, with five slightly darker pink radial stripes, surrounded by small bracts. Flowers in midsummer. Fruits light brown, rounded, ⅛ inch wide. Each fruit contains two seeds that can remain viable in the soil for decades; birds eat the seeds.

Another plant commonly referred to as morning glory is *Ipomoea tricolor*. The seeds of this plant contain ergoline alkaloids and LSA (a precursor to LSD) and are hallucinogenic.

Why You Should Avoid It: Bindweed contains several alkaloids that cause leaves to be mildly toxic. Because these alkaloids are more concentrated in the roots, the roots should be avoided as a food source. However, the root has been used medicinally as a laxative and is said to be strongly purgative. Apparently, the plant can be used as a condiment and as a flavoring in a liqueur called Noyau, but no details are given as to which part of the plant is used for these purposes.

Foxglove

Digitalis purpurea

What It Looks Like: Herbaceous biennial or short-lived perennial. Leaves spirally arranged, simple, 4–12 inches long, 2–4 inches across, covered with gray-white hairs, giving a woolly texture and appearance. In its first year, foliage grows as a basal rosette. Flowering stems develop in the second year, typically 2 feet to more than 6 feet tall. Flowers tubular and pendant, arranged in elongated clusters. Flowers usually purple in color, but some may be pink or white. Inside surface of the flower is heavily spotted. Fruit a capsule that splits open at maturity to release numerous tiny seeds.

Why You Should Avoid It: All members of the *Digitalis* genus contain the glycoside digitoxin. Leaves, flowers, and seeds of this plant are all poisonous and, though mortality is rare, can be fatal if eaten. Extracted from the leaves, this same compound is used medicinally to treat heart failure.

Groundsel

Senecio vulgaris

What It Looks Like: Grows 4–16 inches tall; bears bright yellow florets mostly hidden by green bracts. Leaves lack petioles; 2–3 inches long, about 1 inch wide, alternating along length of the plant, becoming smaller toward top of the plant. Leaf lobes typically sharp to rounded saw-toothed, covered with soft, smooth, fine hairs. Stems hollow. Flowers are open clusters of 8 to 10 small cylinder-shaped rayless yellow flower heads ¼–½ inch with a highly conspicuous ring of black-tipped bracts at base of inflorescence. Root system a shallow taproot. Reproduces by reseeding itself.

Why You Should Avoid It: While this plant was and occasionally still is used medicinally, all species of this genus contain pyrrolizidine alkaloids, substances that with chronic exposure can cause irreversible liver damage in humans.

Lupine

Lupinus polyphyllus

What It Looks Like: Stems erect, hollow, up to five feet tall. Leaves green, palmately compound, divided into 5 to 18 leaflets radiating from a central point; smooth upper surfaces, hairy undersides. Leaves alternate along main stem, well below flowers. Flowers shaped like pea blossoms, primary color bluish-purple, browning with age. Flowers arranged in spikes 12–28 inches long along upper section of main stem. Each flower ⅓–⅔ inch long. Flowers from July to August, with seeds ripening from July to October. Fruits are pods covered with dense hairs. Late in the season, they open on one side and spill their dark, beanlike seeds.

Why You Should Avoid It: The seeds of many lupine species contain bitter-tasting, toxic alkaloids, though there are often sweet varieties within the same species that are safe to eat. Here taste is a very clear indicator. These toxic alkaloids can be leached out of the seeds by soaking overnight, then thoroughly rinsing seeds in a colander. For an added measure of safety, it's wise to change the water once during cooking as well. Fungal toxins also readily invade the crushed seed and can cause chronic illness. Newer garden hybrids of lupine contain quite high concentrations of toxic alkaloids and should never be eaten.

Petty Spurge

Euphorbia peplus

What It Looks Like: Erect, bright green annual growing to 2–10 inches tall with smooth, hairless stems. Stems branched, dividing three to five times. Leaves along stem grow alternately, but upper leaves borne opposite. Leaves pear-shaped to triangular or rhombic. Flower very small and green, surrounded by bracts; flowers difficult to see as they look like new leaves forming at ends of stems. Stems and leaves exude a sticky white sap when broken.

Why You Should Avoid It: This plant, like many in the *Euphorbia* genus, contains toxic diterpene esters. The plant's sap is toxic to human skin and has long been used as a traditional remedy for removal of common skin lesions, including cancer, sun spots, warts, and corns. Not to be ingested.

Poison Hemlock

Hemlock Parsley
Conium maculatum

What It Looks Like: Smooth, hollow stalks with purple blotches and no hairs on stems. Can get quite tall, sometimes up to 8 feet or higher. Leaves finely divided and lacy, overall triangular in shape, up to 20 inches long, 16 inches broad. Flowers small, white, clustered in umbels up to 4–6 inches across. Produces many flower heads in open, branching inflorescence. Starts growing in early spring, producing flowers in late spring. When crushed, leaves and root emit a rank, unpleasant odor.

Why You Should Avoid It: Poison hemlock contains at least eight toxic alkaloids, the most dangerous among them being coniine. Coniine is a neurotoxin that disrupts the central nervous system. Ingestion in any quantity can result in paralysis, respiratory collapse (via paralysis), and death.

Scarlet Pimpernel

Red Chickweed, Poison Chickweed, Poor Man's Weatherglass

Anagallis arvensis

What It Looks Like: Weak, sprawling stems growing to about 20 inches long, bearing opposite, bright green, oval leaves. Small, salmon-colored flowers produced in leaf axils June to August. Flowers open only when sun shines. Square stem, lack of prominent hairs, and reddish flowers distinguish this plant from chickweed.

Why You Should Avoid It: Scarlet pimpernel contains saponins (see Saponins sidebar in chapter 3). Ingestion is not recommended. Also, skin contact with the plant can cause dermatitis in some people. Though it is listed in many sources as toxic, there are also many accounts of the leaves being used raw in salads or cooked as spinach. Also, scarlet pimpernel was once highly regarded as a medicinal herb, especially in the treatment of epilepsy and mental problems, but there are no formal studies to support these uses. Due to the saponins, the pulverized plant is used for washing and bathing in Nepal.

Water Hemlock and Spotted Water Hemlock

Cicuta douglasii and *C. maculata*

What They Look Like: Rhizomatous perennial herb producing a hollow, erect stem to a height of 2½–4 feet. Long leaves made up of several lance-shaped, pointed, serrated leaflets. Each shiny green leaflet 1–8 inches long; entire leaf may be up to 20 inches long. Typically a large swelling at base of stem. Inflorescence an umbel of white flowers similar in appearance to many other species in the carrot family. Fruits tan to brown, less than ¼ inch long. *C. maculata* more common; both species' appearance and smell are very similar to one another. A distinguishing characteristic of *C. douglasii* is that its sap turns reddish-brown when exposed to air.

Why You Should Avoid Them: According to the USDA, water hemlocks are the most violently toxic plants growing in North America. Only a small amount of the plants' toxin, cicutoxin, is needed to produce poisoning in livestock or humans. This toxin acts directly on the central nervous system, producing violent convulsions. It is found principally in the tubers but is also present in the leaves and stems during early growth.

Yew

Western Yew, Oregon Yew, Pacific Yew
Taxus brevifolia

What It Looks Like: Various species of *Taxus* are found in most regions of North America. Pacific yew, native to the Pacific Northwest, a small to medium-size conifer tree, growing 30–50 feet tall with a trunk up to 1½ feet in diameter, occasionally larger. Yews have thin, scaly, brown bark, covering a thin layer of tan sap wood with darker-colored heartwood. Leaves needlelike, lanceolate, flat, dark green, ½–1½ inches long, ¹⁄₁₆–⅛ inch wide, arranged spirally on the stem. However, the leaf base is twisted so needles are aligned in two flat rows on either side of the stem. Female seed cones highly modified, each containing a single seed ⅛–¼ inch long surrounded by a modified scale that develops into a soft, bright-red berrylike structure (aril). Male cones round, ⅛–¼ inch in diameter.

PHOTO BY NICK JOHNSON

Why You Should Avoid It: All parts of the yew, except for the flesh of the berries, are extremely poisonous. The primary toxin is taxine, a cardiac depressant that acts rapidly to cause convulsions and paralysis. There is no known antidote. The chemotherapy drug paclitaxel (taxol), used in breast, ovarian, and lung cancer treatment, is derived from yew.

GLOSSARY

achene: A dry, nonfleshy fruit containing a seed; outer surface is somewhat hard, giving the fruit the appearance of a seed. Such seeds typical of Asteraceae family.

alkaloid: Any of a class of nitrogenous organic compounds of plant origin that have pronounced physiological actions on humans. Includes many drugs (morphine, quinine) and poisons (atropine, strychnine).

alternate: Leaves that grow singly at different levels on the stem, alternating on one side of the stem and then the other.

annual: A plant that completes its life cycle within a single growing season.

anther: Pollen-bearing structure at tips of flower stamens (male reproductive organs). Often appear powdery from grains of pollen.

aril: An extra seed covering, typically colored and hairy or fleshy.

astringent: A sour or bitter flavor. Also a substance that causes the contraction of body tissues, typically used to reduce bleeding from minor abrasions.

basal rosette: Leaves that arise from a central point, usually in a circular shape.

biennial: A plant that completes its life cycle within two growing seasons.

bolt: To flower or produce seeds prematurely or develop a flowering stem from a rosette.

bract: A modified or specialized leaf, especially one associated with a reproductive structure such as a flower. Bracts are usually quite different in appearance from foliage leaves; may be smaller, larger, or of a different color, shape, or texture. Typically, they also look different from parts of the flower, such as petals and/or sepals. Before blooming, bracts form a covering around the flower bud; once the flower has bloomed, bracts remain just below flower and sepals.

bulb: A short, modified underground stem surrounded by usually fleshy modified leaves that contain stored food for the shoot within.

bulblet: Small bulb or bulb-shaped growth arising from the leaf axil or in place of flowers.

burr: A rough or prickly envelope of a fruit that sticks or clings.

calcium oxalate crystals: A chemical compound made from calcium and oxalate that precipitates as a solid crystal. The most frequently found ingredient in kidney stones in the United States. In plants, the needle-shaped oxalate crystals are known as raphides.

calyx: The group of modified leaves called sepals that typically form a whorl enclosing petals and forming a protective layer around a flower bud.

cambium: A layer of tissue beneath hardened bark from which vascular tissue grows by division, resulting in secondary thickening in woody plants.

capsule: A dry fruit that releases its seeds by splitting open when ripe.

central vein: One of the vascular bundles or ribs that form the branching framework of conducting and supporting tissues in a leaf or other expanded plant organ.

composite: Tiny flowers grouped and organized to resemble one large flower. Usually known as disk flowers or ray flowers, depending on shape of petals. All flowers in Asteraceae family are composite flowers.

compound: A leaf that has two or more leaflets; can be either pinnately compound or palmately compound.

conifer: A tree that bears cones and evergreen needle-like or scalelike leaves; includes pines and firs.

cordate: Heart shaped.

corm: A short, thick, solid, underground stem, sometimes bearing papery scale leaves, as in crocus or gladiolus, which stores food.

corolla: The petals of a flower considered as a single unit.

crown: The point from which a plant's shoot or shoots emanate.

cystolith: A mineral concretion, usually of calcium carbonate, occurring in the surface tissues of certain plants.

deciduous: A tree or shrub that sheds its leaves annually.

dentate: Edged with toothlike projections.

disk floret: Small tubular flowers at the center of the flower head of certain composite plants, such as the daisy.

elliptic: A symmetrical, elongated circle; oblong.

epidermis: Outermost layer of cells covering leaves and young parts of a plant.

finely dissected: Leaves that branch repeatedly, such as carrot leaves.

floret: One of the small flowers making up a composite flower head.

frost tender: Perennial plants that cannot withstand frost.

gamma-linolenic acid: A fatty acid found primarily in vegetable oils; sold as a dietary supplement for treating problems with inflammation and auto-immune diseases, but the efficacy of such use continues to be disputed.

glycoside: A compound formed from a simple sugar and another compound by replacement of a hydroxyl group in the sugar molecule. Many drugs and poisons derived from plants are glycosides.

glyphosate: A broad-spectrum systemic herbicide used to kill weeds, especially annual broadleaf weeds and grasses known to compete with commercial crops grown around the globe. Monsanto's trade name for it is Roundup. While glyphosate has been approved by regulatory agencies, there are growing concerns about its increasing presence in drinking water and its effects on humans and the environment.

hardy: Perennial plants that can withstand freezing temperatures and winter conditions.

heartwood: The older, nonliving central wood of a tree or woody plant, usually darker and harder than the younger sapwood.

heavy metals: Toxic metals that can negatively impact human health. In very small amounts, many metals are necessary to support life. However, in larger amounts, they become toxic and may build up in the body to become significant health hazards.

herbaceous: Green and leaflike in appearance and texture, as distinguished from a woody plant.

herbicide: A substance that is toxic to plants and is used to destroy unwanted vegetation. Most commercial herbicides contain chemicals that can be harmful to people, animals, and the environment.

herbicide resistance: The ability of a plant to adapt to a herbicide so it becomes immune to the herbicide. Herbicide resistance in a weed is perceived to be a serious problem in the world of agriculture because the weeds develop more quickly than new strains of herbicide can be developed to combat them.

hydrocyanic acid: Also known as hydrogen cyanide; depending on dosage, can be poisonous. Small amounts are found in pits of almonds, cherries, apricots, and nectarines as well as seeds of apples.

hypanthium: A floral structure consisting of the bases of sepals, petals, and stamens fused together. Typically ringlike, cup-shaped, or tubular; its presence often indicates a member of the Rosaceae, Grossulariaceae, or Fabaceae family.

inflorescence: A cluster of flowers growing from a commen stem.

invasive plant: Introduced species that can thrive in areas outside its native habitat. Often very adaptable; often have a high reproductive capacity. Its vigor combined with a lack of natural enemies often leads to outbreak populations.

lanceolate: Shaped like the head of a lance; oval and narrow, tapering to a point at each end.

lateral: Attached to the side of an organ, such as leaves on a stem.

latex: Milky or clear sap that coagulates on exposure to air; exuded by such plants as dandelion and milkweed.

leaf axil: The small area between a leaf stalk or branch and the stem or trunk from which it is growing.

leaflet: Each of the leaflike structures that together make up a compound leaf.

lobed: Having deeply indented margins (edges).

margin: The edge, as in the edge of a leaf blade.

midrib: A large, strengthened vein along the midline of a leaf.

mucilage: A polysaccharide substance exuded by some plants as a viscous or gelatinous substance.

native plant: Endemic or indigenous to an area.

nitrate: A naturally occurring form of nitrogen found in soil; forms when microorganisms break down fertilizers, decaying plants, manures, or other organic residues. In moderate amounts, nitrates are harmless, and indeed growing plants use them to satisfy nitrogen requirements. However, if there is too much nitrate in the soil, such as with overfertilization or overgrazing, plants cannot metabolize it all and the excess can leach into groundwater. If people or animals drink water high in nitrates, it may cause methemoglobinemia, an illness especially dangerous to infants (blue baby syndrome).

nitrogen fixing: A process by which plants and soil microbes together convert atmospheric nitrogen into water-soluble nitrogen, thereby enriching the soil they grow in. Nitrogen fixing plants are often the first to colonize disturbed soil.

node: The place on a plant stem where a leaf is attached.

nutlet: A seed covered by a stony layer, such as the kernel of a drupe. (Plums, peaches, and cherries are drupes.)

obovate: Egg-shaped and flat, with the narrow end attached to the stalk and the broad end located away from the base.

opposite: Occurring in pairs at the same level on opposing sides of a node. Leaves that sprout from the same position on a branch, usually on opposite sides of the branch.

ovate: Having an oval outline or ovoid shape, like an egg.

oxalate: A term describing salts or crystals derived from oxalic acid. Many metal ions combine with oxalic acid to form insoluble oxalates, a prominent example being calcium oxalate, the primary constituent of the most common kind of kidney stones.

oxalic acid: An acid found in many plants, especially those related to spinach and rhubarb. Can aggravate existing health conditions like rheumatism, arthritis, gout, kidney stones, or hyperacidity.

palmate: A compound leaf divided into several leaflets arising from the same point at the top of the petiole.

palmately compound: Having more than three leaflets attached directly to the petiole. If the leaflets all radiate outward from a common point at the end of the petiole, the leaf is said to be palmately compound.

panicle: A branched, usually elongated inflorescence (cluster of flowers).

pappi: The tuft of hairs on each seed of thistles, dandelions, cat's ear, and similar plants that assists dispersal by the wind.

pedicel: A small stalk bearing an individual flower in an inflorescence.

peduncle: The stalk bearing a flower or fruit, or the main stalk of an inflorescence.

perennial: A plant that lives for more than two years.

pesticide: A chemical used to prevent, destroy, or repel pests including insects, mice and other animals, weeds, fungi, or microorganisms such as bacteria and viruses. Most commercial pesticides contain chemicals that can be harmful to people, animals, or the environment.

petal: Modified leaves that surround the reproductive parts of flowers. Often brightly colored or unusually shaped to attract pollinators.

petiole: The stalk attaching the leaf blade to the stem.

pinnate: Leaflets growing opposite each other in pairs on either side of the stem.

pistil: The female reproductive part of a flower. Centrally located; typically consists of a swollen base, the ovary, which contains the potential seeds (ovules); a stalk (style), arising from the ovary; and a pollen-receptive tip (stigma), variously shaped and often sticky.

pod: A dry, several-seeded capsule that breaks open at maturity to discharge seeds.

potherb: A plant whose leaves, stems, and/or flowers are cooked in a pot and eaten. Also used for plants that are used for seasoning, such as mint.

prickle: Hard structures with sharp, or at least pointed, ends; comparable to hairs but can be quite coarse (for example, rose prickles). Extensions of the cortex and epidermis, whereas thorns are modified branches or stems that usually occur at nodes.

prostrate: Lying flat against the ground.

ray flower: One of the narrow flowers, resembling a single petal, that surround the central disk in a composite flower, such as the daisy or sunflower.

resveratrol: A natural compound found in Japanese knotweed, grapes, mulberries, peanuts, and other plants or food products, that may protect against cancer and cardiovascular disease by acting as an antioxidant, antimutagen, and anti-inflammatory.

rhizome: A thick, horizontal, underground stem of plants such as mint and iris. New roots and shoots arise from buds on the rhizome.

sapwood: The newly formed outer wood located just inside the vascular cambium of a tree trunk and active in the conduction of water.

scaber: Rough.

serrate: Toothed, with asymmetrical teeth pointing forward, like the cutting edge of a saw.

silicle: A short, broad silique occurring in some cruciferous plants.

silique: A narrow, elongated seed capsule peculiar to the Cruciferae family.

sporophyll: a leaf that produces spores.

stamen: The male organ of a flower, usually consisting of a stalk (filament) and a pollen-bearing portion (anther).

stolon: A slender, prostrate, or trailing stem, producing roots and sometimes erect shoots at its nodes.

strobilus: A conelike structure consisting of sporophylls borne close together on an axis, for instance in some club mosses and horsetails.

succulent: Juicy, fleshy; a plant with a fleshy habit.

taproot: The main, descending root of a plant with a single dominant root axis.

tepal: A segment of the outer whorl in a flower that has no differentiation between petals and sepals.

terminal: Situated at the tip or the apex.

thorn: A sharp, stiff point, usually a modified stem, that cannot be detached without tearing the subtending tissue.

trifoliate: A compound leaf of three leaflets; for example, a clover leaf.

tuber: An underground storage organ formed by the swelling of an underground stem that produces buds and stores food; for example, a potato.

umbel: An inflorescence that consists of a number of short flower stalks (pedicels) that are equal in length and spread from a common point, somewhat like umbrella ribs.

woody: A plant having hard, lignified tissues or woody parts, especially in stems and branches.

BIBLIOGRAPHY

Ballerini, Luigi. *A Feast of Weeds: A Literary Guide to Foraging and Cooking Wild Edible Plants.* Berkeley, CA: University of California Press, 2012.

Batdorf, Carol. *Northwest Native Harvest.* Surrey, BC: Hancock House Publishing, 1990.

Benoliel, Doug. *Northwest Foraging: The Classic Guide to Edible Plants of the Pacific Northwest.* Revised and updated ed. Seattle: Skipstone, 2011.

Biala, Danna. "What Are Sources of Resveratrol?" *Livestrong,* April 13, 2011, www.livestrong.com /article/420324-what-are-sources-of-resveratrol/.

Boerboom, Chris, and Michael Owen. *Facts About Glyphosate-Resistant Weeds.* Glyphosate, Weeds, and Crops Group (with BASF, Bayer Crop Science, Dow AgroSciences, Dupont, Indiana Soybean Board, Illinois Soybean Association/Illinois Soybean Checkoff Board, Monsanto, Syngenta, Valent USA, USDA Critical and Emerging Pest Competitive Grants Program, and USDA North Central IPM Competitive Grants Program). www.glyphosateweedscrops.org/Pubs.html.

Borrell, Brendan. "Friend to Aliens: Are Invasive Species Really a Big Threat?" *Scientific American,* February 2011.

Brady, Nyle C. *Advances in Agronomy.* Vol. 34. Waltham, MA: Academic Press, 1981.

Brill, Steve. "Wild Man Steve Brill." www.wildmanstevebrill.com

———. *The Wild Vegetarian Cookbook.* Boston: Harvard Common Press, 2002.

Brill, Steve, and Evylyn Dean. *Identifying and Harvesting Edible and Medicinal Plants in Wild (and Not So Wild) Places.* New York: William Morrow Paperbacks, 1994.

Burns, Diane. *Berries, Nuts and Seeds Take-Along Guide.* Lanham, MD: Cooper Square Publishing, 1996.

———. *Wildflowers, Blooms and Blossoms Take-Along Guide.* Lanham, MD: Cooper Square Publishing, 1998.

Castleman, Michael. *The New Healing Herbs: The Essential Guide to More than 125 of Nature's Most Potent Herbal Remedies.* Emmaus, PA: Rodale Books, 2010.

"Centre—Environmental Living and Training." www .celtnet.org.uk/ Recipes/

Chaudhry, Ozair. "Herbicide-Resistance and Weed-Resistance Management." *Plant Protection, Diversity, and Conservation.* Vol. 2. New Delhi: Biotech Books, 2011.

Cook, Langdon. *Fat of the Land: Adventures of a 21st-Century Forager.* Seattle: Skipstone, 2011.

Couplan, Francois, and James Duke. *The Encyclopedia of Edible Plants of North America: Nature's Green Feast.* New York: McGraw-Hill, 1998.

Craft, David. *Urban Foraging—Finding and Eating Wild Plants in the City.* Memphis, TN: Service Berry Press, 2010.

Crowhurst, Adrienne. *The Weed Cookbook.* New York: Lancer Books, 1972.

Davis, Donald, Melvin Epp, and Hugh Riordan. "Changes in USDA Food Composition: Data for 43 Garden Crops, 1950 to 1999," Bio-Communications Research Institute, PubMed.gov, 2004. www.ncbi.nlm.nih.gov/pubmed /15637215.

Deane, Green. "Eat the Weeds and Other Fun Things Too," www.eattheweeds.com.

Del Tredici, Peter. *Wild Urban Plants of the Northeast.* Ithaca, NY: Comstock Publishing Associates, 2010.

Duke, James A. *Handbook of Edible Weeds.* Boca Raton, FL: CRC Press, 2000.

———. "Phytochemical and Ethnobotanical Database,"

www.ars-grin.gov/duke/.

Eat the Invaders. "Fighting Invasive Species, One Bite at a Time," http://eattheinvaders.org.

Elias, C. *Green Smoothie Recipes and Other Healthy Smoothie Recipes: Discover over 50 Easy Smoothie Recipes.* Seattle: CreateSpace and Cressida Elias, 2012.

Elias, Thomas, and Peter Dykeman. *Edible Wild Plants: A North American Field Guide to Over 200 Natural Foods.* New York: Sterling, 2009.

Fallon, Sally, and Mary Enig. *Nourishing Traditions.* Washington, DC: New Trends Publishing, 1999.

Fogg, John M. Jr. *Weeds of Lawn and Garden.* Philadelphia: University of Pennsylvania Press, 1946.

Foster, Steven, James A. Duke, and Roger Tory Peterson. *A Field Guide to Medicinal Plants and Herbs of Eastern and Central North America.* Boston: Houghton Mifflin Harcourt, 1999.

Gibbons, Euell. *Stalking the Wild Asparagus.* Chambersburg, PA: Alan C. Hood & Company, 2005.

Green, Jared. American Society of Landscape Architects. "An interview with Nina-Marie Lister on her book Ecological Urbanism," *The Dirt: Connecting the Built Environments,* June 5, 2012, http://dirt.asla.org/2011/06/07/interview-with-nina-marie-lister/.

Hahn, Jennifer. *Pacific Feast: A Cook's Guide to West Coast Foraging and Cuisine.* Seattle: Skipstone, 2010.

Hertzberg, Ruth, Janet Greene, and Beatrice Vaughan. *Putting Food By,* 5th ed. New York: Penguin Group, 2010.

Holmes, Hannah. *Suburban Safari: A Year on the Lawn.* New York and London: Bloomsbury Publishing, 2006.

Jenkins, Virginia Scott. *The Lawn: A History of an American Obsession.* Washington, DC: Smithsonian Books, 1994.

Johnson, John A. "Cui Bono, Human Behavior Unpacked: Freedom and Control" *Psychology Today,* April 30, 2011. www.psychologytoday.com/blog/cui-bono/201104/freedom-and-control.

Jones, Pamela. *Just Weeds: History, Myths and Uses.* Boston: Houghton Mifflin, 1994.

Kallas, John. *Edible Wild Plants: Wild Foods from Dirt to Plate.* Layton, UT: Gibbs Smith, 2010.

———. "Wild Food Adventures," www.wildfoodadventures.com/northcarolina.html.

Kaufman, Rachel. "Urban Foragers Cropping Up in U.S." *National Geographic's Green Guide,* September 3, 2010, http://blogs.nationalgeographic.com/blogs/thegreenguide/2010/09/urban-foragers-cropping-up-in.html.

Lee Scott, Timothy. *Invasive Plant Medicine: The Ecological Benefits and Healing Abilities of Invasives.* Rochester, VT: Healing Arts Press, 2010.

Lerner, Rebecca. "First Ways." www.Firstways.com.

Lewis-Stempel, John. *Foraging: The Essential Guide to Free Wild Food.* London: Elliot Right Way Books, 2012.

Livestrong.com. "Nutritional Value of Wild Foods Versus Cultivated Foods." www.livestrong.com/article/366071-nutritional-value-of-wild-foods-verses-cultivated-foods/

Mabey, Richard. *In Defense of Nature's Most Unloved Plants.* New York: Ecco, 2011.

Madison, Deborah. *Preserving Food without Freezing or Canning.* White River Jct, VT: Chelsea Green Publishing, 2007.

Montgomery, David. *Dirt: The Erosion of Civilizations.* Berkeley, CA: University of California Press, 2007.

Peterson, Lee Allen, and Roger Tory Peterson. *A Field Guide to Edible Wild Plants: Eastern and Central North America.* Boston: Houghton Mifflin, 1978.

Pimentel, David. "Environmental and Economic Costs of the Application of Pesticides Primarily in the United States." Cornell News Release, 1999. www.news.cornell.edu/releases/jan99/species_costs.html.

"Plant-Lore," www.plant-lore.com

Plants for a Future, http://pfaf.org

Poe, Melissa. "Foraging Wild Foods in Urban Spaces." Institute for Culture and Ecology, http://ifcae.org/projects/urbanforaging/

Pojar, Jim, and Andy MacKinnon. *Plants of the Pacific Northwest Coast: Washington, Oregon, British Columbia & Alaska.* Edmonton, AB: Lone Pine Publishing, 2004.

Rascio, N., and F. Navari-Izzo. "Heavy Metal Hyperaccumulating Plants." *PubMed, October 16, 2011.* www.ncbi.nlm.nih.gov/pubmed/21421358.

Robbins, John. *Healthy at 100: The Scientifically Proven Secrets of the World's Healthiest and Longest Lived People.* New York: Ballantine Books, 2007.

Runyon, Linda. *Eat the Trees!* Dorchester, MA: Wild Food Company, 2011.

———. *The Essential Wild Food Survival Guide.* Dorchester, MA: Wild Food Company, 2009.

Savage, Sunny. "Wild Food Plants." http://wildfoodplants.com

Shaw, Hank. *Hunt, Gather, Cook: Finding the Forgotten Feast.* Emmaus, PA: Rodale Books, 2012.

Squire, David. *Foraging: Self-Sufficiency.* New York: Skyhorse Publishing, 2011.

Stewart, Amy, and Briony Morrow. *Wicked Plants: The Weed That Killed Lincoln's Mother and Other Botanical Atrocities.* Chapel Hill, NC: Algonquin Books, 2009.

Thayer, Samuel. *The Forager's Harvest: A Guide to Identifying, Harvesting and Preparing Edible Wild Plants.* Birchwood, WI: Forager's Harvest Press, 2006.

———. *Nature's Garden: A Guide to Identifying, Harvesting, and Preparing Edible Wild Plants.* Birchwood, WI: Forager's Harvest Press, 2010.

US Department of Agriculture. "Plants Database," www.plants.usda.gov

———. "USDA National Nutrient Database for Standard Reference," http://ndb.nal.usda.gov

US Department of the Army. *The Illustrated Guide to Edible Wild Plants.* New York: BN Publishing, 2009.

Warren, Piers. *101 Uses for Stinging Nettles.* London: Wildeye, 2006.

Wigginton, Eliot, and the Foxfire Fund. *Foxfire 2.* New York: Anchor Press, 1973.

———. *Foxfire 3.* New York: Anchor Press, 1975.

INDEX

ABOUT THE AUTHOR

After 22 years as an environmental policy analyst, Melany Vorass Hererra retired to pursue a combination of two of her greatest loves: plants and food. An avid forager for well over 40 years, she now enjoys teaching urban foraging workshops to a wide variety of audiences. Smack in the heart of Seattle, she and her husband tend an urban farm with chickens, honeybees, and goats. Between urban foraging, farming, trapping, and fishing—as well as canning, drying, and fermenting—her family's food, Melany seldom needs (or has time) to visit a grocery store. Melany holds a degree in environmental studies with an emphasis in ethnobotany from the Evergreen State College. She also has a permaculture design certificate from Oregon State University. Her website is www.frontyardforager.com.